SEASONS OF GRACE

Seasons of Grace

Reflections from the Christian Year

JAMES F. KAY

WILLIAM B. EERDMANS PUBLISHING COMPANY
GRAND RAPIDS, MICHIGAN

Copyright © 1994 by Wm. B. Eerdmans Publishing Co.

255 Jefferson Ave. S.E., Grand Rapids, Michigan 49503

Printed in the United States of America

00 99 98 97 96 95 94   7 6 5 4 3 2 1

Library of Congress Cataloging-in-Publication Data

Kay, James F., 1948-
Seasons of grace: sermons through the Christian year / James F. Kay.
p.   cm.
ISBN 0-8028-0783-6 (pbk.)
1. Church year sermons. 2. Sermons, English — Australia.
3. Sermons, American. 4. Reformed Church — Sermons. I. Title.
BV4253.K38   1994

252'.6 — dc20   94-34550
CIP

*For the Congregation
of Toorak Uniting Church
Melbourne, Victoria
Australia*

Contents

CONTENTS

Foreword

Good preaching, like skillful windsurfing, is a risky and rapid-paced balancing act done at the confluence of many forces. The preacher paddles bravely through the currents into the theological depths and waits. Suddenly, and almost always unexpectedly, the wave of a biblical text swells commandingly, and the preacher rises on its crest, ever at peril of pitching over into the roiling sea, urgently adjusting the tautness of the sail to catch the unpredictable wind of the Spirit. At once thrilled and terrified, the preacher rides the surge toward the people gathered on the shoreline, some heedless, many curious, some amused by the strange sight, a few expectantly hopeful.

Jim Kay is a nimble pulpit windsurfer. He is humbled by the power of the sea, but he is not afraid to brave the wind and the waves, and, in these sermons, one can feel the power of the swirling energies that give vitality, direction, and strength to courageous and effective preaching.

Unlike many contemporary sermons that wade in the safe shallows, these sermons have theological depth. The meaning of Jesus Christ, the power of the Holy Spirit, the communion of the saints, the role of Mary, the resurrection, and the second coming — these are among the many-fathomed doctrines that give substance and size to Jim Kay's preaching. These sermons harness the power of the surging wave, not merely the foam.

The sermons in this volume have depth, but they also have

range. Not content to allow his preaching to fall into a single, predictable pattern, Jim Kay allows the flow of text and occasion to summon a variety of voices, moods, and language styles. He teaches; he sings; he paints pictures; he tells stories. Some of the sermons in this collection drive their claims home like a drumbeat; others soar deftly through the imagination on metaphorical breezes. Here he speaks in street dialect, there in the careful prose of the theologian. Here he beckons us forward to hear his stories; there he summons us far out beyond the sight of land to explore the exotic reefs of apocalyptic.

So, we should read these sermons, savor them, and read them again. We should read them as models of effective preaching, but, even more, read them as compelling invitations to catch the next wave ourselves, to feel the wind and spray in our own faces, and to experience anew the transforming adventure of the Christian faith.

Thomas G. Long
Princeton Theological Seminary

Introduction

During Lent and Eastertide of 1993, while on research leave from Princeton Theological Seminary where I teach preaching, I served as Visiting Minister of Toorak Uniting Church in Melbourne, Australia. I have my doubts whether teachers of preachers need themselves to preach anymore than I would expect a theater critic, like Frank Rich, to perform on the Broadway stage. The roles of the critic, coach, or teacher require their own reflective skills that are distinct from those of the performer, player, or preacher. Nevertheless, there is nothing that informs the teaching of preaching more than the actual practice of the pulpit ministry of the Word. My own teacher of preaching, James A. Forbes, used to say that preachers not only need to be "called," they need to be "re-called"! I wish to thank the congregation of Toorak Uniting Church and their minister, James Donaldson, for graciously "re-calling" me from the classroom to their distinguished pulpit; Ian and Judith Roach for their generous underwriting of this exchange; and President Thomas W. Gillespie and Vice President Frederick W. Cassell of Princeton Theological Seminary for their enthusiastic support of this venture.

The eighteen sermons in this volume are grouped according to the Christian year, and half of them, including all of those listed under Lent, Holy Week, and Eastertide (with the exception of "The Lion and the Lamb"), were preached in

INTRODUCTION

March, April, or May 1993 at the Toorak Uniting Church. Five other sermons were also originally preached in local congregations: "Mary's God — and Ours," on December 22, 1991, at Madison Avenue Presbyterian Church, New York; "Joseph," in December 1974, at Northern Lakes Parish, Beltrami County, Minnesota; "A Labor Not in Vain," on September 9, 1990, at Setauket Presbyterian Church, Setauket, Long Island, New York; "Who Is My Mother?" in May 1985, at Plymouth Church of the Pilgrims, Brooklyn, New York; and "Burnout — and Beyond," on June 22, 1986, at Lafayette Avenue Presbyterian Church, Brooklyn, New York.

Four sermons were preached in academic settings: "The Coming Cloud," the title and germ of which I used with permission from Christopher Morse, on August 6, 1989, at Princeton University Chapel (for Morse's further reflections on this apocalyptic theme, see his *Not Every Spirit: A Dogmatics of Christian Disbelief* [Valley Forge: Trinity Press International, 1994], pp. 329-34); "All the Way Down," on January 11, 1992, at the Fifth Calvin College Symposium on Worship and Church Music, Grand Rapids, Michigan; "The Lion and the Lamb," in the spring of 1983, at James Chapel, Union Theological Seminary, New York; and "It Does Not Yet Appear," on October 29, 1991, at Miller Chapel, Princeton Theological Seminary.

"Lord, Give Us the Word!" was originally preached on June 18, 1991, before the Presbytery of the Palisades meeting in Hackensack, New Jersey.

I gratefully acknowledge permission granted by the editor of *The Princeton Seminary Bulletin* to reprint versions of the following sermons: "The Coming Cloud," "Mary's God — and Ours," "A Labor Not in Vain," and "John 3:16."

Unless otherwise indicated, biblical citations are from the Revised Standard Version.

Princeton, New Jersey   James F. Kay

ADVENT AND CHRISTMAS

The Coming Cloud

"And then they will see the Son of Man coming in a
cloud with power and great glory." (Luke 21:27)

Think for a moment of a cloudless sky — not just for a week,
or even a month, but for a *whole year* — or two — or three!
How we would pray and, yes, even dance for a rain cloud!

So in the days of Elijah, during the great national apostasy
under King Ahab and Queen Jezebel, "there was no rain in
the land" (1 Kings 17:7). Only when a bone-dry nation finally
fell on its face before the Lord God did the longed-for cloud
come.

The First Book of Kings tells how that cloud took shape
off Israel's Mediterranean coast. At first, just a wisp as small
as a human hand appeared in the sky. Then more clouds began
to gather. The day turned dark. The wind rose up, and sheets
of rain fell on the parched, cracked earth.

So in the days of Elijah, a cloud came in the shape of a
hand and stretched out its blessings from an open heaven.

But, as you know, coming clouds do not always bring such
blessings. Scarcely more than fifty years ago, in 1939, the clouds

3

were gathering — war clouds. Adolf Hitler was demanding the annexation of Danzig and the Polish Corridor into his Third Reich. Meanwhile, on these shores, some 350 American women gathered at the New York World's Fair. There amid the marvels of "The World of Tomorrow," these women declared to the world of that day their unanimous opposition to sending American boys to fight in another European war. These women were all mothers, Gold Star Mothers. They had already sacrificed their children to the First World War.[1]

But nothing these mothers said and nothing the diplomats did could avert what Winston Churchill later called "the gathering storm." And so the war came.

And the war did not end until the coming of another cloud at 8:15 A.M. on August 6, 1945. An eyewitness recalls: "The sky was serene, the air was flooded with glittering morning light. . . . The sirens and also the radio had just given the all-clear signal. . . . A blinding flash cut sharply across the sky. . . . [my] skin . . . felt a burning heat. . . . [A] violent rush of air pressed down my entire body. . . . I raised my head, facing the center of Hiroshima. . . . [There I saw] an enormous mass of clouds . . . [they] spread and climbed rapidly . . . into the sky. Then its summit broke open and hung over horizontally. It took the shape of . . . a monstrous mushroom."[2] A physicist blinded by that same cloud later wrote, "Everything seemed dark, dark all over. . . . Then I thought, 'The world is ending.'"[3] A novelist later remembered thinking she was witnessing "the collapse of the earth which I had read about as a child."[4] Amid the rubble, the housekeeper at the Jesuit mission

---

1. News of the Christian World, *Christian Century*, 17 May 1939, p. 651. On the New York World's Fair of 1939, see Steven Rea, "Back to the Future," *Applause* (August 1989): 21-23.

2. Robert J. Lifton, *Death in Life: Survivors of Hiroshima* (New York: Random House, 1967), pp. 18-19.

3. Ibid., p. 22.

4. Ibid., pp. 22-23, quoting Yoko Ota, *Shikabane no Machi* (Town of corpses) (Tokyo: Kawade Shobo, 1955), p. 63.

cried out over and over again, "Shu Jesusu, awaremi tamai!" "Our Lord Jesus, have pity on us!"[5]

And since that brilliant August 6, the poison mushroom cloud threatens to come again at almost any time.

The coming cloud: Will it be a cloud like the one for which Elijah prayed — a cloud that blesses the earth and her people like an outreached hand? Or will it be a cloud that smothers the world with death? Which will it be? Can we forecast the future?

There are those who claim we can. There are those who say we can know the shape of our future and even control our future by spotting present trends.

Recently, that distinguished scientific journal, *Life* magazine (which you probably hide under your *Smithsonians*!), devoted some thirty pages to what the twenty-first century holds for a "typical" American family: "By the year 2000 half of the new homes will be substantially computerized. . . . While you're out, your house continues to perform programmed tasks: Start the dishwasher and water the garden . . . open gates to a certain delivery truck, activate household noises to deter burglars. Commands can be changed via telephone — if you're ahead of schedule, call home to adjust temperature and humidity levels, turn on the sauna, feed the cat." Video screens, we are told, will "provide security (the computer can distinguish you, regular guests, and pets from intruders), though kids might object to the electronic eyes that will allow parents to monitor Junior doing homework. When it's time for bed, go right upstairs. The house will let the cat in and turn off the lights."[6]

In the twenty-first century, food as we know it will be a thing of the past. Meat, for example, "will be ninety-nine percent fat free, reconstituted to look like London broil or sirloin. In fact, it will be something like sawdust glued together

---

5. John Hersey, *Hiroshima* (New York: Alfred A. Knopf, 1958), p. 18.
6. "Visions of Tomorrow," *Life,* February 1989, p. 62.

with alginate of kelp." If you find this less than appetizing, *Life*'s editors quickly add, "Fear not — we tried it, and it was fantastic."[7]

Yes, we have tasted the future, and it's "fantastic"!

We can now forecast what is coming: the bright, silver clouds of the future will open up the blessings of technology.

Or will they?

Present trends hold the key to the future?

Well, what do you make of trends like these: ozone vanishing over the polar ice caps; the greatest mass extermination in sixty-six million years of the earth's flora and fauna carried out by a fairly new species called *Homo sapiens;* tropical rain forests disappearing at one hundred acres per minute; seventy-five hundred dead dolphins washing up on our Atlantic coast two summers ago, and medical wastes still closing our beaches.

Facts like these are bandied about almost daily on the airwaves and newsprint. Never has Paul's description of a creation groaning for redemption seemed so apt (Rom. 8:22).

Life magazine may regale us with the computerized house of the future, but other forecasters question whether our future will even be fit for habitation.

So present trends are ambiguous. Some point to paradise. Others lead to the gates of hell. And even now clouds are gathering on the horizon of the future. Can the Bible give us the forecast? Can we know about the coming cloud? Will it bring nourishing blessing, or will it be a pillar of fire that rains unimaginable destruction? Which will it be?

Some parts of the Bible seem to give a fairly direct answer: repent and all will be well. That's what happened in Elijah's day. Israel turned away from God. So God shut up the heavens. And the drought came. Then the famine came. When Israel turned back to God, back to the morality and religion of Moses, God opened the heavens and showered the land with blessing. Isn't this the old-time religion we hear on radio

---

7. Ibid., p. 58.

and TV? If America will only repent and return to the Christian faith, God will bring us showers of blessing. But if we forsake God, God will forsake us. We will be overwhelmed by disaster.

But even the Bible recognizes that things are not quite that simple. The rain, Jesus tells us, falls on both the just and the unjust (Matt. 5:45). And the Bible, too, recognizes that terrible things often cloud the careers of good and upright people. Good King Josiah, who recovered and honored the Torah, is cut down by Pharaoh's army (2 Kings 23:29). The Book of Daniel remembers the many righteous martyred for their faith (Dan. 11:33-34). And outside the gates of Jerusalem, a young rabbi in whom no fault was found screams from his Roman cross, "My God, my God, why hast thou forsaken me?" (Mark 15:34).

If the gospel is good news, it is not because it predicts a bright, shiny future based on our morality or piety. The gospel is neither a cocoon that insulates us from the sufferings of this present age nor a pair of earplugs that shuts out the groaning of creation. And the gospel is not a tranquilizer to quell the cries of Gold Star Mothers and all other modern Rachels who weep for their children because they are no more.

The gospel is good news, not because it *predicts* a future based on our good behavior or other present trends; the gospel is good news because it *promises* a future based on God's faithfulness to Jesus Christ.

This same Jesus, who cried in agony from his cross of suffering, this same Jesus is coming toward us on the horizon of the future, "coming in a cloud with power and great glory."

And because the future belongs to Jesus Christ, because Jesus Christ has a future, we who belong to him, whose lives are entwined with his by baptism and faith, we will have a future with him.

That is why we can never give up — on ourselves, on our friends, on our enemies, or on our world! If the future were not Jesus Christ but simply the sum total of present trends,

7

what despair would overwhelm us! But because Jesus Christ is our ultimate future, we have a hope and a peace that the world can neither give nor take away.

We do not deny that on earth nations are in agony. We do not deny that ecological collapse appears imminent. We do not deny that scores are choked with fear. But Jesus says, "Now when these things begin to take place, look up and raise your heads, because your redemption is drawing near" (Luke 21:28).

We are not to cower in fear of the future.

We are not to crouch, like a boxer, in doctrinaire defensiveness.

We are not to flee from solidarity in suffering into privatized spirituality.

We are to stand erect, confident, hopeful, knowing that *whatever cloud comes to meet us, faith will see the face of Jesus Christ.*

And so this morning I leave you not with a prediction but with a promise. I cannot forecast the future. Whether the coming cloud brings us the bounty of heaven itself or whether it brings instead "tribulation, or distress, or persecution, or famine, or nakedness, or peril, or sword," who can say? As a minister of the gospel, I can only proclaim to you its promise that no future, however beclouded, "will be able to separate us from the love of God in Christ Jesus our Lord" (Rom. 8:35, 39).

Therefore, "look up and raise your heads . . . your redemption is drawing near."

Mary's God — and Ours

Luke 1:39-56

I heard it first on CNN Headline News. So perhaps it's true. The other morning, over breakfast, there on TV was an excited, bleached-blond woman, about forty I'd guess, bundled in a winter coat. She was telling the reporter she had just "seen Mary," the Blessed Virgin Mary — seen her, right there. Now mind you, this was not in some Polish village, or at a popular Mediterranean shrine, or in some remote Mexican town with an unpronounceable Aztec name. No, this ordinary, middle-aged American had just seen the Virgin Mary in Denver, of all places. "I don't know *why* she appeared to *me*. *I* am not important. I am only Mary's instrument. Yes. I saw her."

In this cable age of ours, word spreads fast. Hordes are now trooping daily to a shrine outside Denver where Mary is currently appearing. They keep vigil with rosary beads and Polaroid cameras. They elbow past souvenir hawkers and TV journalists. They're straining, all straining, to glimpse the Virgin. With Elizabeth of old, they too are chanting: "Blessed are you among women, and blessed is the fruit of your womb!" (Luke 1:42).

Of course, the official church is embarrassed by all the fuss. I phoned a friend of mine, a priest, out in Ridgewood, New Jersey.

"Anthony, have you heard the news? The Blessed Virgin is appearing in Denver." Detecting Presbyterian glee in my question, Anthony snorted, "Well, if she is, Jim, I wish she would just go away. We have the church and the sacraments — what more do we need?"

Yes, we have the church and the sacraments — not to mention the Holy Spirit. What more do we need?

But still the Virgin keeps visiting Czestochowa, Lourdes, Fátima, Guadalupe, and now Denver.

The odd thing about these multiple appearances of Mary is just how rarely she actually appears in the pages of our Bible. The apostle Paul never mentions Mary's name. Mark's Gospel, perhaps our oldest, skips the birth of Jesus altogether. Mary, with Jesus' brothers, does make an appearance in Mark 3:31, but Jesus seems indifferent to her presence. True, the Gospel of John (19:25-27) puts Mary at the foot of the cross. But this same Gospel also finds Jesus rebuking Mary when his mother mentions at Cana that wedding guests have run out of wine (2:4). My colleague, Beverly Roberts Gaventa, points out that "apart from this one scene in John, only Luke narrates words spoken by Mary."[1] Only Luke. But even in Luke, where Mary finally talks, the focus is not really on *Mary*, but on her *God*. She exalts the God of Abraham, she exults in the God of Israel. Even in Luke, the focus is not really on Mary, but on her God.

No doubt many are seeking Mary today. And, perhaps, some are really finding her. But do they find Mary's God? If the Mary they seek is the one shown to us in Luke's Gospel, then the real question is where do we find Mary's *God*?

Who is her God anyway?

In the Magnificat, Mary tells of her Savior who has "looked

---

1. Gaventa, "A Place for Mary in Protestant Preaching?" *Journal for Preachers* 14, no. 4 (1991): 35.

with favor on the lowliness of his servant" (Luke 1:48, NRSV). Lowliness. The Greek behind our English word is not talking simply about the humility of Mary, but about her poverty, her low station in life, her abject condition. Like so many pregnant, teenage girls in our cities, Mary belongs to what we now call the underclass. John Calvin commented, "In the eyes of the world she was of no account, and she rated herself no higher."[2] But this little one, this wretched one, this lowly one, this one, God raises up!

But Mary's God is not her God alone. Oh, no. Mary sings a freedom song on behalf of all the faithful poor in the land. She sings a freedom song for all the poor and the powerless who in their wretchedness still believe that God will make a way for them.

Despite all the evidence, and against all the odds, Mary rejoices (Luke 1:46-55, NRSV): She tells of the God who "has scattered the proud in the thoughts of their hearts"; the God who "has brought down the powerful from their thrones, and lifted up the lowly"; the God "who has filled the hungry with good things, and sent the rich away empty"; the God of Abraham and Israel who is faithful to his promises. Mary's God is the God who keeps faith with faith, who remembers the least and the last and the lowly. Mary's God is the God who dethrones the rich and the proud, who reverses fortunes — economic and political — who makes a way for the faithful poor where no way can be found. This is Mary's God, the God of Jesus Christ.

I have to confess that Mary's God sounds mighty radical and awfully revolutionary. The Magnificat is not easy to sing when we busy our lives with what we have, or with "those in the know," or with what we can steal. Is it really possible for

---

2. *A Harmony of the Gospels: Matthew, Mark and Luke,* Calvin's New Testament Commentaries, vol. 1, ed. David W. Torrance and Thomas F. Torrance, trans. A. W. Morrison (Edinburgh: Saint Andrew Press, 1972; reprint, Grand Rapids, Mich.: Wm. B. Eerdmans, 1980), p. 35.

us to worship Mary's God here this morning? Can Mary's God really be *our* God?

Please understand. I am not accusing. I am confessing. After all, I work in Princeton, New Jersey! And I am so rich and so comfortable and so insulated from "the sufferings of this present time" (Rom. 8:18) that I can only confess that Mary's song sticks in my throat.

Oh, yes, I have the church and the sacraments. After all, I'm a minister, they're in my portfolio. What more do I need?

Well, if I'm to sing Mary's song and to believe in Mary's God, I may just need Mary's help. I'm not talking about a supernatural vision. Well, not exactly. But I do need vision, a renewed vision of the coming of God's will and way on this earth and in this land. I need to hear and to see those who are poor, "for yours," says Jesus, "is the kingdom of God"; I need to hear and see those "who are hungry now, for," says Jesus, "you will be filled"; and I need to hear and see those "who weep now, for," says Jesus, "you will laugh" (Luke 6:20-21, NRSV). In the voices and faces of these least and last, we may just hear and see the witness of Mary.

This week, I think I caught a glimpse of her. I read Joelle Sander's riveting interviews, *Before Their Time: Four Generations of Teenage Mothers.*[3] One of the mothers Joelle Sander interviews is Louise Eaton, an African American of some eighty-six years. Louise is one of thirteen children. She used to work alongside her daddy cutting tobacco and shucking corn down in St. Mary's County, Maryland. When she was only sixteen, she had to get married. Her husband, William, a short-order cook, was an alcoholic. Eventually, he and Louise separated. But Mrs. Eaton supported herself and her daughters by taking in as many as ten youngsters at a time in her modest six-room house in Queens, New York. Even during the Great Depression, Mrs. Eaton never went on welfare and, with her

---

3. Sander, *Before Their Time* (New York: Harcourt Brace Jovanovich, 1991). The quotations that follow are taken from pp. 68-69 and 175-76.

second husband's pension, managed to pay off her home mortgage.

But Mrs. Eaton can testify for herself:

> "Darlin' . . . I know what God tells me from the Bible. He has blessed me. . . . I'm blessed. . . . When I was a child, if I didn't have somethin' to eat on my table . . . I would take my little basket to a neighbor's house and he would give me apples, potatoes, greens. He'd give me cabbage. You don't find that today. All those poor people lying in the streets. I saw a lady with six children outside on the pavement. How can children grow up like this? You know, God put aplenty in this world for all of us, and when you elect a President . . . you want him to *care* for the poor. . . . People can't work for $3.50 an hour anymore. Maybe you can get something to eat, but how could you pay these rents today? . . .
>
> "God has taken care of me. I have carried out his wishes, been good to people, and He has always rewarded me with his kindness."

Joelle Sander comments, "From the time I first met this energetic and generous woman, she has downplayed her troubles. She speaks more about her gratitude than of her great struggles. Clearly, she never thought she would get as much as she has received in life, and she never forgets to thank God for her well-being. . . . 'He has done it all for me.' . . .

"Characteristically, Mrs. Eaton speaks of two important goals she still looks forward to achieving. 'I want to learn how to play the guitar. . . . And I want to live to be one hundred and ten years old! I have no intention of dying before that. I'm having too good a time' [and this] despite her swollen ankles and diseased leg."

The last thing Joelle Sander and Mrs. Eaton spoke about was the manner in which Mrs. Eaton wants to be buried: "I want to be laid out in my nice white dress, and I don't want hundreds of flowers. No, that's a waste of money. . . . That money should go to the poor."

And Mary said,

"He has brought down the powerful from their thrones and lifted up the lowly.

"He has filled the hungry with good things and sent the rich away empty."

"Darlin' . . . when you elect a President . . . you want him to care for the poor."

And Mary said,

"He has looked with favor on the lowliness of his servant."

"Darlin' . . . God has taken care of me. I have carried out his wishes, been good to people, and He has always rewarded me with his kindness."

And Mary said,

"My soul magnifies the Lord, and my spirit rejoices in God my savior."

"Darlin' . . . He has done it all for me. . . . I want to live to be one hundred and ten years old! I have no intention of dying before that. I'm having too good a time. . . ."

Though CNN did not report it, I saw Mary this week. I heard anew her freedom song, her song of praise and prophecy, from the earthy and angelic Mrs. Eaton out yonder in Queens.

And when Advent turns to Christmas, and when I get back to Princeton, I too want to sing once more with Mary, and the whole company of heaven, "Glory to God in the highest!"

Glory to God whose will shall be done on earth as it is in heaven!

Glory! Glory to God! To Mary's God — our God — forever and ever! Amen!

Joseph

Matthew 1:18-25

In our Gospel lesson this morning from Matthew, the gift of Christmas — the sheer miracle of its message — is that in Jesus Christ, God is Emmanuel — with us and with us always. In Jesus Christ, a particular concrete life, God comes all the way down and enters our world. The Word becomes flesh. God becomes human. This is the holy mystery of Christmas.

We normally look at child development in terms of heredity and environment — especially in all that the parents bring to a child — or fail to bring to a child. But nothing in Joseph adequately accounts for the Christ. Joseph is not the star of the Christmas story! We carol the Christ Child, the Blessed Virgin, the shepherds, the wise men, and Luther even has us singing how "the cattle are lowing." But how often do you hear a Christmas carol, or any hymn for that matter, that so much as mentions Joseph's name? Mary and even Pilate make the Apostles' Creed, but not Joseph!

As Matthew's narrative opens we find that Mary and Joseph are an engaged couple. Under Jewish law, they are

15

legally married, even though no formal wedding has taken place. But Mary becomes pregnant during her engagement to Joseph, but not by Joseph. Under these circumstances, Joseph should divorce Mary. The normal procedure would be for Joseph to initiate court proceedings. Mary would be charged with adultery. Can you picture Joseph's agony? Mary has betrayed his trust. Her private affair will soon become public scandal. Mary will face legal judgment. If spared, she will bear the stigma of social condemnation.

Was Joseph filled with anxiety? or anger? Whatever feelings brooded over him, he finally comes to his decision. As a good Jew, he will keep the law. He will divorce Mary. But as a good Jew, Joseph is also a man of mercy. While he decides to divorce Mary, he will do it quietly, out of court. He will lovingly spare his fiancée public humiliation. It's a compromise. Joseph will keep the law's divorce requirement, but he will temper it with mercy. Having made his decision, he sleeps on it. And while Joseph sleeps,

> an angel of the Lord appeared to him in a dream, saying, "Joseph, son of David, do not fear to take Mary your wife, for that which is conceived in her is of the Holy Spirit; she will bear a son, and you shall call his name Jesus, for he will save his people from their sins." (1:20-21)

The angel announces the virgin birth in the Gospel of Matthew to overcome Joseph's decision to divorce Mary. The impact of the Incarnation displaces Joseph as the actual father and, by cancelling Joseph's decision to divorce Mary, enables him to become Jesus' legal father. God's sovereign presence overrides conventional convictions. God enables Joseph to reframe the whole mess in a new messianic way. Mary's child is the deliverer of Israel.

Normally it was the responsibility of a Jewish father to choose his child's name. But, again, the Incarnation overrides this traditional male prerogative. Joseph is told, not asked, what to call the boy: "You shall call his name Jesus, for he will save his people from their sins." The child is named by God himself through his messenger. Since Joseph has no share in begetting the child, he has no share in naming the child. Joseph only gives him the name God gives him: Jesus, "Savior."

The Incarnation — this incredible "impossibility" — that God should become human, that God should *want* to become human — marks the story of Christmas. Just as a meteor plummeting into the crust of the moon displaces millions of tons of rock, so the impact of God entering our world displaces the human participants in Matthew's drama. From the standpoint of Christian faith, there is just no adequate way to account for this interruption we call "Jesus Christ." When God becomes human, the impact of this event rearranges the usual roles and the usual expectations.

Through men and women who, like Joseph, step aside in faithful obedience, the God of Christmas still works today. Through such ordinary folk the extraordinary news of Christ is often borne.

A few years ago, amid all the publicized controversies of a typical Presbyterian General Assembly, a presentation was made by an Eskimo delegation from the North Slope of Alaska. These indigenous peoples possessed no recognized governmental unit at the very time the oil companies were laying the trans-Alaska pipeline. They wanted to form a borough to levy taxes for public schools. They contacted the church. They secured a loan of about $150,000 to organize their government. A year later, they came to the General Assembly. They repaid their loan and made a further gift to the church for the self-development of other peoples.

What was not widely known was that behind the scenes there was a "Joseph," in fact, a "Josephine!" For decades, a woman missionary labored among these Alaskans to translate Christian literature into their own language. As a result, the impact of the gospel for good spread well beyond the church.

So at Christmas let us remember and give thanks not only for the Christ Child and the Virgin Mary but also for the "Josephs" and the "Josephines" whose dreams still prepare the way of the Lord.

SUNDAYS AFTER
EPIPHANY

All the Way Down

Now when all the people were baptized, and when Jesus also had been baptized and was praying, the heaven was opened, and the Holy Spirit descended upon him in bodily form like a dove. And a voice came from heaven, "You are my Son, the Beloved; with you I am well pleased." (Luke 3:21-22, NRSV)

As a Presbyterian, I generally run with the church crowd. My particular church crowd is affluent, educated, and overwhelmingly white. Worship on Sunday is the Republican Party at prayer — except, of course, for the ministers! My church crowd is pretty reserved. Some Sundays only two or three venture to greet me. I wonder if these warm souls are visitors themselves — or perhaps former Methodists! Civility and gentility describe my Sunday morning crowd.

But a few months ago, I found myself in another crowd. I sat in Madison Square Garden. It was fight night. And what a crowd it was! Seventeen thousand of them. Rough, rowdy, rude. Few coats and ties here. Lots of T-shirts and gold chains. Amid the whistles and catcalls, a seminarian, David Brat, said to me, "You know, lately you Presbyterians talk a lot about evangelism. But face it. You wouldn't *want* any of these people in your churches." And you know, *that* Brat is right! An unruly New York fight crowd is hardly our crowd, is it?

But Luke is not so standoffish. Luke's Gospel overflows with crowds. In almost every chapter, Jesus is surrounded by crowds. Sometimes they're reverent; sometimes they're rough — trampling over each other. But they welcome him. He teaches them. They follow him. He feeds them. Crowds, throngs, multitudes.

That's how it is with Jesus from the very beginning. In the fifteenth year of the reign of Tiberius Caesar, Pilate judges Judea and Herod governs Galilee. But "multitudes," we are told, "multitudes" follow another voice into the wilderness. They come in droves. They come driven to hear and to see a prophet named John preaching "a baptism of repentance for the forgiveness of sins" (Luke 3:3).

Whose crowd is this anyway? Can we glimpse their faces? Mark isn't much help. He describes them in generalities as "all the country of Judea" and "all the people of Jerusalem" (1:5). With similar hyperbole, Matthew also throws in "all the region about the Jordan" (3:5). And so described they come: *all* Judea, *all* Jerusalem, *all* of Jordan, all crowding night and morning into the wilderness.

Whose crowd is this? Matthew numbers in this throng both Pharisees *and* Sadducees (3:7). In *this* crowd we see *both* the idealists who keep Israel's law and the realists who keep their Roman masters happy. But together they march, these patriots and parasites, trudging to the Jordan. And with them come publicans and prostitutes (cf. Matt. 21:32) and "soldiers" (Luke 3:14), presumably Jewish security officers, possibly in the pay of Herod himself. What a crowd now gathers at the river. The pious and the profane, in blue collars and white. What a sight. This human horde, this motley crew, this "brood of vipers," all snaking to Jordan's shore. Fight night and Sunday morning squeezing together into God's kingdom. "And they were baptized by [John] in the river Jordan, confessing their sins" (Mark 1:5).

And there in the water stands Jesus. He went along with the crowds. He jostled his way to the Jordan side by side with all the rest. Luke puts it this way: *"Now when all the people were baptized, and when Jesus also had been baptized. . . ."* Jesus did not stand far off. He did not disdain them. He came all the way down with them into the Jordan. He stands in the mire and the muck, shoulder to shoulder, with prostitute and Pharisee, soldier and Sadducee, standing in solidarity with all who confess their sins. With them, he too receives a baptism of repentance for the forgiveness of sins.

His sins? Jesus confessing his sins? What kind of a Savior is this? Such solidarity in sin, such solidarity with sinners shocks us. It shocked John the Baptist. Matthew reports, "John would have prevented him, saying, 'I need to be baptized by you, and do you come to me?'" (3:14).

And we would prevent him as well. We look at the crowds we run in, or more often, the crowds we run from, and we say, "Oh, Jesus, you don't really want to get too close to that bunch." And so we imagine Jesus' baptism as a kind of role-playing, sort of playacting.

You may have watched on CBS recently as Tyne Daly convincingly portrayed the plight of a homeless woman. But if Tyne Daly really wanted to become a homeless person, her producers and her fans would surely try to prevent her. "It's just a role, Tyne. You're an actress. You're not really one of them." "No, Jesus. You're not one of *us*. You're too good for the likes of us. Defer to your best interests. Turn back from this path." But Jesus will not turn back from us, for he is not playacting.

Yes, "John would have prevented him." And so would we all. But what we are bent on preventing, God is undertaking.

The Scriptures express this amazing grace in many ways: Isaiah writes, "[He] was numbered with the transgressors" (53:12); Paul declares, "For our sake [God] made him to be sin who knew no sin" (2 Cor. 5:21); and the Philippian hymn sings of Christ Jesus who "emptied himself, taking the form of a slave" (2:7).

Karl Barth comments, "No one who came to the Jordan was as laden and afflicted as He. No one was as needy. No one confessed his sins so sincerely, so truly as his own. . . . He does not stand at a distance from the sin of others. . . . He bears it as His own in order to bear it away."[1]

The sinlessness of Jesus is found in his utter solidarity with sinners, however pious, however profane. This is hard for me to understand. I don't understand the baptism of our Lord. I don't understand why Jesus wants to get more than his feet wet with crowds of sinners like me — and unlike me. But Jesus will not be prevented. What we would prevent, in our piety and profanity, God has already accomplished. God is even now bone of our bone and flesh of our flesh. God is even now Emmanuel — with us. For God's Beloved has come all the way down to the Jordan. Jesus Christ has been baptized with us and for us, confessing our sins as his very own. He bears them as his own to bear them all away.

And God is pleased . . . "well pleased."

---

1. Barth, *Church Dogmatics*, vol. 4, pt. 4, *The Christian Life*, ed. G. W. Bromiley and T. F. Torrance, trans. G. W. Bromiley (Edinburgh: T. & T. Clark, 1960), pp. 59-60.

A Labor Not in Vain

Therefore, my beloved . . . be steadfast, immovable, always abounding in the work of the Lord, knowing that in the Lord your labor is not in vain. (1 Cor. 15:58)

How can Paul sound so sure?

How can he say and how do we know that a minister's labor, or our own work at whatever task, will not be in vain?

Doesn't our experience of work really suggest the opposite? Don't we have doubts as to whether anything we accomplish comes to very much in the end?

Amid the tennis defeats at Forest Hills yesterday, do Paul's upbeat words really comfort a Steffi Graf or a Boris Becker? — not to mention a John McEnroe! Or, turning to the tragic, how in the pillage of Kuwait do Paul's words ring true for the tens of thousands who have lost their life's savings, their homes, and their jobs — not to mention their country? And would Paul still sound so triumphant facing the Watkins family now back home in Provo, Utah, the family whose twenty-two-year-old son, Brian, was stabbed to death in a

Manhattan subway station when he came to the defense of his mother? At a news conference this week, the family appealed for justice saying, "Please don't let Brian die in vain."[1]

Yet in the face of all the evidence, recent and ancient, of what Samuel Johnson called "the vanity of human wishes," Paul does not join the preacher of Ecclesiastes in declaring that "all is vanity." No, Paul dares to affirm "that in the Lord your labor is not in vain."

Frankly my first response to Paul's affirmation is simple: Has this man ever worked in a church? Seen days lost to trivia? Toiled with a stubborn copying machine? Sat through endless committee meetings? Counseled with couples going through the motions? Stood in courthouses, and hospitals, and cemeteries, where nothing he said would change the outcome? Labor not in vain?

Is Paul simply blind to the obvious?

Is his faith a *tour de force* that ignores the facts?

Or is he practicing a little rhetorical bravado — swaggering for a moment before the steamroller of reality?

Paul was not always so certain his labor was not in vain. Four or five years before he first wrote to the Corinthians, he was having an anxiety attack over the Thessalonians (cf. 2 Cor. 11:28). The church in Thessalonika had not been easy to organize in the first place. In fact, Paul's missionary efforts provoked such an outcry that he was run out of town. Paul was worried sick that in his absence new converts to Christ might abandon the church. So Paul finally sent his associate, Timothy, to check out the situation. Paul explained to the Thessalonians, "When I could bear it no longer, I sent to find out about your faith; I was afraid that somehow the tempter had tempted you and that *our labor had been in vain*" (1 Thess. 3:5, NRSV; emphasis added).

"Please, God," we can almost hear Paul pray, "Please, God, don't let my labor be in vain."

---

1. *New York Times*, 7 Sept. 1990, sec. B4.

Paul was called to proclaim the gospel. Paul was an apostle. Paul had seen the risen Lord. But none of this kept him from the real anxiety that among the Thessalonians his labor had been in vain.

And the call to pastoral work does not shield us either from the anxiety that our labor, too, is in vain. Indeed, pastoral work often leads us into temptation, the temptation to despair, to wonder if we are of any use, to suspect that our work for the Lord is in vain.

One young pastor felt that temptation when, despite his counsel, a battered wife took her malnourished baby and went back to her abusive husband.

Another pastor, not long out of seminary, heard the tempter mocking in a courtroom as a senile judge awarded custody of an eight-year-old boy to a psychopathic father with a penchant for guns.

And I, too, have heard the tempter's voice as I trembled at the graveside of a teenager whom I befriended, and baptized, and confirmed, but who, nevertheless, apparently took his own young life.

In the face of incidents like these, does not every true pastor fear with Paul that he or she has labored in vain?

How do we go on? How do we walk and not faint? For we know that the church will not always be as affirming of us as it is at the moment of our installation.

How can we overcome the temptation to despair, to wonder if we are of any use? How can we embrace the strong affirmation that "in the Lord your labor is not in vain"? How do we move with Paul from the anxiety of 1 Thessalonians to the confidence of 1 Corinthians?

Well, pick up almost any religious periodical these days, and you will find all sorts of paths offering to lead you from anxiety to confidence. Ministers are constant targets for all sorts of schemes claiming to renew their confidence or their ability to manage their recalcitrant congregations.

For example, the National Association of Clergy Hypnotherapists can train you in hypnotically induced relaxation techniques. If despite your best efforts membership declines, Religion in American Life and the Advertising Counsel advise that "a warm, human approach may be the way to go in getting people to come to church." Feeling lackluster? A congregation in northeastern Pennsylvania suggests a more aggressive tack. It advertises for an associate pastor with "entrepreneurial instincts." No doubt I, and many other ministers, could benefit from hypnotically induced relaxation. No doubt I could be "warmer" and more "human." And no doubt I could learn to do with more entrepreneurial "umph."

But is this the gospel in which we stand? Up on the confident platform of the world's wisdom with our hypnotherapy, warm smiles, and entrepreneurial instincts? On this platform you will hear no discouraging word of labor that is in vain — certainly not before packed churches managed by relaxed, confident entrepreneurs!

How very much this emerging American model of ministry would have appealed to the Corinthians. I doubt, before Paul wrote to them, they had ever needed assurance that their labor was not in vain.

After all, they had caught the Spirit. How else could they boast about their new natures?

They were into the new age movement of wisdom and spirituality. How else had they transcended what is material and corruptible?

They were already singing, "O death, where is thy sting?" (15:55). They were highflyers. They spoke in the tongues of angels (13:1). How could their faith and practice be in vain?

But Paul warns them as he warns us. No matter how impressive all the religious talk and techniques, boosterism is not the power of the gospel. For according to Paul, we can secure neither our labor nor our lives from vanity. Only God can do that, and God does it only through a *cross*.

So Paul's move from anxiety to assurance that in the Lord our labor is not in vain is not the trick of a "confidence man."

28

It is rather confidence in the God of the gospel who comes all the way down. The God who is no stranger to our own despair. Yet while we were helpless, this God overcame all that overcame Jesus on his cross. This is God's work. And in Jesus Christ, God promises to overcome all that will overcome us — in life and in death. This is God's Word.

This week, when the Watkins family met with the press after Brian's subway murder, Brian's brother, Todd, fought back tears. Todd explained how his brother's killing had not altered his family's faith in God: "We don't know the answers," he said. "All we know is God lives."

How do we move from anxiety to assurance that our labor is not in vain? We make this move with Paul, and with Todd Watkins, and with Christians in every time and place because when we least expect it, when there is no evidence for it, *those who twist in agony with Christ on the cross bring back the only word that can secure our labor: "God lives."*

Therefore, my beloved sisters and brothers, "be steadfast, immovable, always abounding in the work of the Lord, knowing that in the Lord your labor is not in vain."

LENT

The Light of the World

John 9

❧   ❧

God's light is shining in the face of Jesus Christ. God's light is shining at times we do not expect, in places where we would scarcely venture. God's light is shining on those we often cast into outer darkness.

Walt was a sixteen-year-old street tough in Brooklyn, New York. "My parents," he remembers, "were good people, but they didn't have much money. We looked out our windows on streets smelling of garbage. I went to school every day, but I was illiterate. Like most of my friends, I joined a gang . . . I became its leader."

One evening Walt stood with his friends in Prospect Park. They were waiting to fight a rival gang that never showed. As he and his friends walked out of the park they saw a man preaching right there on the street corner. "He was saying how God loved us and could forgive us and how life could change. We started mocking him because there was nothing better to do. I never saw that man again," Walt recalls. But later that evening, "I was overwhelmed by a presence that I didn't even know enough to call Christ. . . . [That night] I fell into a deep sleep, during which I dreamt that the garbage outside my window had turned into roses. When I awoke, I knew my future would be different."[1]

That's the testimony of the Reverend Dr. Walter Ungerer, pastor of the First Presbyterian Church in Kokomo, Indiana. "I was overwhelmed by a presence that I didn't even know enough to call Christ." "And who is he, sir, that I may believe in him?" (John 9:36). God's light is shining in the darkness.

When we least expect it.

Before we even have a name for it.

The light is shining on those slated to be cast out.

Exposing the garbage.

Restoring purpose.

Bestowing sight.

Turning all that is rotten into roses.

"One thing I know, that though I was blind, now I see" (v. 25).

The light has come into the world, praise God! But the light has come into the world in ways we would hardly expect, so we are not always sure that the light is of God.

Yes, "we know that this man is a sinner" (v. 24). Only a beggar, it seems, can get through the scandal: "Whether he is a sinner, I do not know; one thing I know, that though I was blind, now I see" (v. 25). But that, too, now becomes a scandal. That the light and life of God should be seen by a blind beggar, or a gang leader, long before we do, we who bear the name of "Christian."

According to the Gospel of John, the coming of the light, of the will and way of God enfleshed in Jesus Christ, triggers a crisis and brings division into this world: "Those who do not see . . . see; those who see . . . become blind" (v. 39). Jesus

---

1. See Barbara A. Chaapel, "Into the Heart of Faith," *The Princeton Spire* 31, 3 (Summer/Fall 1992): 10ff. I have freely paraphrased this article.

destabilizes and desacralizes the status quo. He threatens the establishment, and so the establishment begins to close ranks.

Isn't that the way it is when more light breaks forth in the church? In recent years, women in increasing numbers have been claiming that they are called by God to the ministry of Jesus Christ. And so what happens? A crisis. And then the old order whose security is threatened goes into crisis management.

We shall hold hearings (v. 13).

We shall find Bible verses (vv. 16, 28, 29).

We shall call witnesses (v. 18).

And we shall cast these upstarts out (v. 34).

Whether in John's Judea of yesteryear or in Dr. Cameron's Sydney of this past week, we shall cast them out![2]

But will we see the light shining in the face of Jesus Christ?

Am I suggesting that the church must always honor the demands of anyone claiming to see the light? Does anything go in today's church? Are there no doctrinal or moral tests for membership, for ordination? Are we blindly to believe everything said from the pulpits, classrooms, and courts of the church? Of course not!

In fact, in the First Letter of John, a tract that emerges from circles similar to those of the Gospel of John, Christians are commanded, "Do not believe every spirit, but test the spirits to see whether they are of God" (4:1).

But how does this testing proceed? It proceeds by the rule of love given to us by Jesus Christ. Whatever in Christian teaching is consistent with the love of God and the love of neighbor belongs to the light. Whatever in Christian teaching is inconsistent with the love of God and the love of neighbor belongs to the devil — even if such teaching, like Satan, can quote Scripture chapter and verse.

----

2. On March 18, 1993, Dr. Peter Cameron, principal of St. Andrew's College, Sydney University, was found guilty of heresy by a presbytery of the Presbyterian Church in Australia. The charge of undermining the authority of the Bible stemmed from his advocating the ordination of women.

Love has a look.

    Love has a story.

        Love has a name: Jesus Christ, who loved us
        and gave himself for us.

And the story of his mission, death, and resurrection is a story of a love that comes all the way down to meet the likes of us, when we least expect it, when we don't deserve it.

As John tells the story, love bends near the earth
    to wash the disciples' feet (John 13:1-12);
        to write in the sand, while a woman's accusers
            slink away (8:1-11);
        and love even bends near the earth to spit on the
            ground, making clay to heal eyes blind from
            birth (9:1, 6).

We honor the Scriptures and call them holy because of their story of love drawing near to us with all its amazing grace. We honor the Scriptures because they tell the story of the God of Jesus, the God of Israel, the God of light in whom there is "no darkness at all" (1 John 1:5).

We read from the Scriptures not as we read citations from a telephone directory or from the criminal code, but we read them in the very light of the old, old story of love stooping low even before we know enough to call upon Christ: "Who is he, sir, that I may believe in him?" (John 9:36).

This light we do not create.

    This light we cannot control.

        This light we can only reflect in our words
        and by our deeds.

It is the light of the glory of God
    bending near to us
        in the face of Jesus Christ.

Life before Death

"Lord, if you had been here, my brother would not have died. . . ." Jesus said to her, "I am the resurrection and the life . . ." (John 11:21, 25)

Jesus was too late: "Lord, if you had been here, my brother would not have died."

Did Martha, and then Mary, say these words with reproach and anger, or with dismay and disappointment? After all, Jesus was four days too late! In Lazarus's case, it was not just a matter of missing the village parson. It was a matter of missing the light of life! Too late.

"Jesus, it's been four long days. The grave dug. The body wrapped. Lazarus buried. The tomb sealed. It's too late."

"Perhaps, Jesus, you would be kind enough to utter a few words *at the grave.*"

"Lord, if you had been here our brother would not have died." Too late!

We live in a world and at a time that wants God, but only on its own terms and in the sweetness of its own time. Yes, we want light and life and, as one newspaper ad puts it, "Immediate Enlightenment." We want it *all*. And we want it all *now*. We're even willing to pay the going rates as long as we see some results.

And we want to enlist Jesus in our planning and plotting, as long as he behaves himself, in accordance with our standard timetable. We'll even grant him top billing as long as he meets our deadlines.

But Jesus is not easy to co-opt. Not because he is against us, but because he, above all, is so deeply for us in ways beyond our calculations.

This is one of the themes of the Gospel of John. At Cana in Galilee, Jesus' mother remarks to him, "They have no wine." And Jesus says to her, "O woman, what have you to do with me? My hour is not yet come" (2:4). In the temple at Jerusalem, Jesus' imminent arrest is put off. Why? John tells us, "His hour had not yet come" (7:30; 8:20). God's timeliness on our behalf is not simply the reflex of our needs, or of our desires, or of our finger snapping. God is neither our sergeant-at-arms nor our garçon standing by for our summons.

God's life only comes to light at the hour of God's own choosing.

And so Jesus tarries. But his delay in reaching Lazarus is not the cringing of life before the inevitability of death. Jesus' delay in coming to the home of Mary and Martha is not a denial of death. For the Gospel of John knows that death is not imaginary. Death is so real it stinks. Jesus' delay in coming to his beloved friends at Bethany is precisely so that life can confront death, that life can come before death.

The story of the raising of Lazarus, unique to the Fourth Gospel, is John's way of narrating that Jesus is indeed the resurrection and the life. Here in Lent we are now given a clue about Easter. The resurrection of Jesus is not just something that happens to Jesus. The resurrection of Jesus is an event that embraces us, that remakes our destiny, that re-creates us as the people of God, that extends to all who believe in Christ. Among the many meanings of the story of Lazarus is surely this clue about Easter: the resurrection is not just something that concerns Jesus; it is something that extends to all who believe in him as the resurrection and the life.

Jesus comes into the world on God's time
    and with God's timeliness.

Jesus comes into the world when the mourners are already hired and the morticians are already paid.

Jesus comes into the world when all human possibilities are at an end, a dead end.

For left to its own time, the world is as hopeless as Lazarus's tomb. There he lies, like the world, in utter darkness. There he is, and there we are —

    taped tight
        shut up
            put away
                put down —

with no exit, no light, no life.

The good news of the gospel for all in such dire straits is Jesus' word to Martha: "I am the resurrection and the life; he who believes in me, though he die, yet shall he live, and whoever lives and believes in me shall never die" (John 11:25-26). Long after the world's time for us has run out, Jesus' hour for us is come.

It is not too late! The One who is the resurrection and the life comes even to us, even in this hour, clothed with his word of promise. For John's Jesus tells us, "Truly, truly, I say to you, he who hears my word and believes him who sent me, has eternal life. . . . Truly, truly, I say to you, the hour is coming, and *now is*, when the dead will hear the voice of the Son of God, and those who hear will live" (5:24-25; emphasis added).

There is a wake-up call this morning for the dead.

LENT

Do you hear it in this hour —
    in this hour of God's own choosing?
      in this hour of life before death?
   "Lazarus, come forth!"
And the one who was dead came forth.

HOLY WEEK

Prophet, Priest, or King?

And when he entered Jerusalem, all the city was stirred, saying, "Who is this?" (Matt. 21:10)

Yes, Jerusalem was shaken, shaken up, and shaken to its foundations. As Jesus emerges into the city, from rumor and anonymity into high-profile visibility, all of Jerusalem is thrown into turmoil. "Who is this?"

I

"And the crowds said, 'This is the prophet Jesus from Nazareth of Galilee'" (Matt. 21:11). The prophet, so they said.

A prophet is a person called by God, called to proclaim the Word of God and to interpret events in the light of God's will and way. But prophecy had virtually disappeared by Jesus' day. For the most part, prophecy only existed in prophetic *books.* But that was long ago. True, there was John the Baptist. But Herod had taken care of him. No wonder Jerusalem was shaken to its foundations. A prophet — once more

— not just on the banks of the Jordan but in Jerusalem, the capital itself!

Many people who saw and heard Jesus believed that he was a prophet. Matthew reports that Herod, the tetrarch, the son of Herod the Great, wanted to put Jesus to death, but "he feared the people, because they held [Jesus] to be a prophet" (14:5). Again, as Jesus preaches during the last week before his execution, the chief priests and Pharisees start to arrest him, but they can't quite pull it off, "because [the multitudes] held him to be a prophet" (21:46). And doesn't Jesus see himself as a prophet when rejected by his hometown of Nazareth? He says, "A prophet is not without honor except in his own country and in his own house" (13:57). Surely, when the crowds of Palm Sunday acclaim Jesus as the prophet they are hailing him with the honor Nazareth refused him.

Yes, Jesus is a prophet, for he preaches that we must do the will of his Father who is in heaven (7:21; 12:50). Yes, he is a prophet who proclaims in preaching and parable the new world of God's reign, the kingdom of heaven. Yes, he is a prophet, for Jesus, too, will be killed (23:29-39).

But then again, Jesus is *not* a prophet! He is not simply a forerunner of the kingdom, like John. He is its fulfiller. He is not simply a witness to a righteous and holy God. He is Emmanuel — God with us. In Jesus, a righteous and holy God draws near even to us. So near he can forgive sins.

Who is this? He is a prophet — but more. He touches and heals real sinners. He is the forgiving Word he bears.

II

Is Jesus, then, more a priest than a prophet? For in Matthew's account of the triumphal entry, Jesus not only shakes the city to its very foundations, but he is an earthquake who rolls through the temple precincts, overturning business-as-usual and confounding the establishment. There is turmoil in the financial markets this morning where the forgiveness of sins has been sold for centuries. Jesus takes charge of the temple, if only for a moment, right in the court of the Gentiles: "[he] drove out all who sold and bought in the temple, and he overturned the tables of the money-changers and the seats of those who sold pigeons" (21:12). What's going on here?

In the outer court of the temple, one found everything needed for animal sacrifices: oxen, sheep, goats, pigeons. Buying and selling. Offering and haggling. The money-changers, the currency exchangers of their day, converted coins into the temple coinage so that pilgrims could pay the temple tax and buy the pigeons for their sacrifices to God.

All of these arrangements were necessary to maintain worship at the temple. But by expelling the merchants and the money-changers, Jesus overturns more than tables. He overturns the whole system of animal sacrifices. He assumes the prerogatives of God's high priest.

Who is this unsettling all Jerusalem? Is this not our high priest who makes the house of God a place of prayer once more?

On the street in front of this building, you will often see a sign, "Church Open Today for Prayer." Our medieval ancestors would have found such a notice strange. What else is a church for? I suppose there are days when no one prays here. But a church open for prayer is a symbol that amid all our traffic and trafficking,
    all the hustle and bustle,
        the getting ahead and the putting it over,
    there is yet a place and a space
        where troubled hearts
          and uneasy thoughts
        can turn to our High Priest in prayer.

Jesus, our priest? Our high priest? Not if by "high" you mean far removed from our hurts and our hearts. For the Letter to the Hebrews says of Jesus, "We have not a high priest who is unable to sympathize with our weaknesses, but one who in every respect has been tempted as we are, yet without sin" (4:15). The writer continues, "In the days of his flesh, Jesus offered up prayers and supplications, with loud cries and tears, to him who was able to save him from death, and he was heard for his godly fear [better, 'in his anxiety']. Although he was a Son, he learned obedience through what he suffered; and being made perfect he became the source of eternal salvation to all who obey him, being designated by God a high priest after the order of Melchizedek" (5:7-10). Do you know fear as you face the future?

Jesus knew fear. He knew anxiety.

He trembled before the cross.

Our high priest has been there,

in our dark nights.

He is there, with us, for us. And he is able — able to sympathize, able to steady us in every storm and trial.

And this high priest, whose house is a house of prayer, is not only the sacrificer but the sacrifice: "he entered once for all into the Holy Place, taking not the blood of goats and calves but his own blood, thus securing an eternal redemption" (9:12).

Jesus in his full humanity gives himself completely without reservation. He is not simply a victim, but he offers himself on the cross. As Jesus approached death, the curtain of the temple was torn in two (Luke 23:44-46). This beautiful curtain veiling the entrance to the Holy of Holies, separating the divine from the human, was torn in two. Jesus, as the final sacrifice, opens the way to God — once and for all.

Who is this? This is Jesus our high priest who intercedes for us, who brings God to us, and whose house shall be called a house of prayer.

III

But on that first Palm Sunday when Jesus entered the City of David, he was also hailed by the crowds in the streets and the kids in the temple as you have hailed him this morning, "Hosanna to the Son of David!" (Matt. 21:9, 15).

Who is this? This is Jesus, the Son of David, the King of Zion.

We often use the proper name Jesus Christ as if "Christ" were Jesus' surname. But really it's his title. Jesus — the Christ — the anointed one — the Messiah — the King of Israel (cf. 1 Sam. 9:16; 24:6).

But can we really claim Jesus as the Christ, as the Messiah?

On that first Palm Sunday wide segments of Judaism held out hope that someday God would restore the kingdom of David (cf. Ps. 2:6-7; 2 Sam. 7:12ff.). The prophets like Jeremiah (30:8-9), Ezekiel (37:21-24), and Zechariah (9:9) all looked forward to this restoration. There would come forth a new king, a political figure, to renew the nation.

No wonder occupied Jerusalem was quaking in its boots on this Sunday. Street demonstrations. Seditious slogans. Disturbances in the temple. Young people chanting, "Hosanna to the Son of David." Could it be here and now before our very eyes the hated Romans would be driven back to the sea?

And so when Jesus is finally arrested and interrogated, the high priest, Caiaphas, says to him, "Tell us if you are the Christ, the Son of God" (Matt. 26:63). Just tell us. If Jesus answers, "Yes," he is guilty of treason under Roman rule. If Jesus says, "No," he will disappoint the crowds who hailed him. He gives an evasive answer: "You have said so" (v. 64). Jesus is not at all comfortable with the title Christ, because he is aware of the nationalistic and political overtones. He is certainly not the Messiah if you mean by that a monarch ruling Israel and dominating her neighbors.

This temptation to seize political power was very real for Jesus. Immediately after his baptism, he was tempted to take this political route. Showing him "all the kingdoms of the world and the glory of them" the devil said to him, "All these I will give you, if you will fall down and worship me" (Matt. 4:8-9). But Jesus turns aside from the path of a political Messiah and chooses instead a crown of thorns.

He enters Jerusalem
    as the Son of David,
not on a war horse
    but on a donkey,
not in military escort,
    with swords drawn and standards raised,
but with crazy civilians
    greeting him with branches,
welcoming him in peace.

Yes, Jesus is the Christ, the Messiah, the King, but only on his terms. He is the Messiah, but only in the sense that his real battles were not with Pilate, or with Caiaphas, or with the money-changers. Jesus' real battles were with the power of this age which is passing away. Jesus' real battles were with the love of power and the fear of power, which still holds good people in its death grip. And so today, Jesus' real battles are not with church leaders, or politicians, or with the movers and shakers. Jesus' real battles are with the power that presumes to control them, to control us, and with the naked power plays that ride roughshod over human community and God's good creation. Jesus' real battles are with every power that refuses to bow before the power of love.

This Palm Sunday Jesus comes again into our city and into this temple. He comes not to oppress us with the love of power but to confront us again with the power of love.

Who is this?

This is Jesus: God's prophet, our priest, our king. To him be the power and the glory! Hosanna in the highest!

John 3:16

For God so loved the world that he gave his only begotten Son, that whosoever believeth in him should not perish, but have everlasting life. (John 3:16, KJV)

Did you memorize John 3:16 as a kid? Who didn't back in the 1950s when Sunday schools were thriving? I memorized it in good Protestant fashion in the language of the old King James Version.

John 3:16. Despite all the cultural ground shifting under our feet, isn't it still the most famous, and perhaps most beloved, text in all the Bible?

And that's just the problem.

When the Christian message is reduced to a sentence, instead of heard as a story, it's so easy for that sentence to become a magic formula or mesmerizing mantra.

I've seen it happen.

John 3:16 turns up repeatedly at professional football games and other televised sporting events. It often appears just as the wide receiver completes a forward pass by carrying the football over the goal line into the end zone for a touchdown. Right?

In short, when that happens in the stadium, six big points go up on the scoreboard. At that moment TV cameras and photojournalists all train their lenses on the end zone.

And something else is often captured in the process. Something you may not see until the photo appears on the next morning's sports page. There in the background, some spectator is holding up a cardboard sign for all the world to see. And on it is printed, "John 3:16," just as the cameras click.

They don't even bother anymore to write out the words. Only the reference appears on the sign. If we can just get the code number, it seems we've got the gospel. That's always a temptation when the Christian message is taken for a cipher instead of a story.

For us more sedate types who would never think of arranging photo-opportunities for God, John 3:16 presents us with yet another problem. It is so engraved in our memory, so beloved, and so familiar we're sure we already know what it means even before we hear it.

Isn't that the way it is with a lot of church chat and preacher talk? We've heard it all before, and frankly, we're bored. We've heard it all before, and so we never really *hear* it. The gospel of God's love has become so familiar and so user friendly that we are no longer amazed by its majesty or its mercy.

That's why the Christian message can only get through to us by sometimes taking the form of a bizarre story. And John alludes to just such a story right before he comes on to what we call "3:16."

> As Moses lifted up the serpent in the wilderness, so must the Son of man be lifted up, that whoever believes in him may have eternal life. (John 3:14-15)

What's that all about?

Well, John is alluding to one of the strangest stories in all Scripture, from the twenty-first chapter of the Book of Numbers. The people of Israel, wandering in the wilderness,

> became impatient on the way. And the people spoke against God and against Moses, "Why have you brought us up out of Egypt to die in the wilderness? For there is no food and no water, and we loathe this worthless food." Then the LORD sent fiery serpents among the people, and they bit the people, so that many people of Israel died. And the people came to Moses and said, "We have sinned, for we have spoken against the LORD and against you; pray to the LORD, that he take away the serpents from us." So Moses prayed for the people. And the LORD said to Moses, "Make a fiery serpent, and set it on a pole; and every one who is bitten, when he sees it, shall live." So Moses made a bronze serpent, and set it on a pole; and if a serpent bit any man, he would look at the bronze serpent and live. (vv. 4-9)

Now that *is* bizarre! A tall tale indeed. No wonder we prefer safe slogans to strange stories. And what in the world does this serpentine story have to do with John 3:16? And what could it possibly have to do with us?

Just this: *When the gospel of God's love is lifted up among us, it draws out all of our venom and all that poisons the world.* The glory of God's eternal love for you, for me, and for the world only touches the earth through a cross — amid the vipers and the venom.

In the Gospel according to John the Son of Man does not ascend after Easter in a cloud of glory. No! For John, the Son of God is lifted up, but only a few feet off the ground on a cross planted in a snake pit.

And from his cross where he reigns, Christ is still speaking on this Lord's Day in Lent, and he is saying to all of us:

Let it go.
  Let it all go.
    Let all the venom go.
Let everything that poisons our lives,
    that corrupts our community
and demeans our humanity,
    let it go.
      Let it all go.
Could this be what it means to be drawn again to Christ?
Could this be what it means to look on the cross and to believe
in him who loved us and gave himself for us?
  To let go of all the stored up venom
      that is killing us,
        just to let it go.
You see, the good news from John's point of view is that Christ
can take it all;
  all the years of stored up venom.
    Christ can take all the bitterness,
      and bear it all away.
From John's point of view, God doesn't wait for us to get well
before paying us a house call. Our situation is too grave for
such gentility. God is already here, where God loves to be,
with the poisoned and the perishing.

  When we hear John 3:16, through the story of the snakes
and the cross, we can do one of two things. We can either look
away from the cross and, bottling up all the poison that is in
us, simply perish; or, looking to the cross and letting loose our
deadliest venom, we can begin to live anew.

  So let it go. Let it all go. Let all the venom go! For the
promise of the gospel story is this:

  For God so loved the world that he gave his only begotten
  Son, that whosoever believeth in him should not perish,
  but have everlasting life.

Thanks be to God!

EASTERTIDE

The Unexpected Easter

John 20:1-18

I

The resurrection was unexpected; on that the Gospels agree. That's why there was no official delegation of disciples on hand to greet Jesus. There was no receiving line. No spruced up little girls in their Easter hats holding ribboned bouquets. And there were no Palm Sunday crowds. Mary Magdalene came to the tomb — alone — and in the dark. She did not come to Jesus' grave expecting anything more than a body.

There are some situations that are not going to get any better. And there's nothing we can do about it. In Mary's case, there was no court of appeal. In Mary's case, there was no way to rectify the death of Jesus. For it was the officers of justice and the upholders of morality who had put him to death.

Now as she walks towards the tomb in the darkness, her heart sinks deeper. The grave has been disturbed. The stone is moved. The body is missing. No doubt the grave robbers and the vandals have already done their dirty work. On that morning, did Mary feel as our Jewish friends may feel when, fifty years after the Holocaust, their cemeteries are still being vandalized and spray painted with swastikas? Is there really no limit to human indecency? In the darkness, Mary weeps.

And in her affliction, "she turned round and saw Jesus standing, but she did not know that it was Jesus" (John 20:14).

For the resurrection was unexpected. On *that* the Gospels agree.

II

She did not know that it was Jesus. But Jesus knew that it was Mary, Mary Magdalene. Who is she?

John reports that she stood at the foot of the cross with Jesus' mother, his aunt, and one unnamed disciple whom Jesus loved (19:25-26). Outside of a few fleeting references in the passion narratives, the only other scrap of information about this Mary comes from the eighth chapter of Luke in this description of Jesus' mission: "he went on through cities and villages, preaching and bringing the good news of the kingdom of God. And the twelve were with him, and also some women who had been healed of evil spirits and infirmities: Mary, called Magdalene, from whom seven demons had gone out . . ." (vv. 1-2).

To say folks were demon possessed was a way of acknowledging in Jesus' day that there are destructive patterns and powers that can overwhelm us and take us captive. Today we have other, more clinical terms for these demons: blind rage, binge drinking, bulimia and anorexia, behaviors both obsessive and compulsive. Whatever affected Mary, she had been out of herself, out of control, perhaps morally, perhaps mentally, perhaps medically, perhaps all three. Then Jesus came.

And on the first day of the new creation, to whom does our risen Lord speak? The first name our risen Lord utters is not "Peter" or "James" or "John" — but "Mary." For the first person to whom the risen Lord appears is Mary Magdalene. And it is not Peter or James or John but Mary Magdalene who first tells the good news we call the gospel: "I have seen the Lord" (John 20:18). How unexpected!

If I were Jesus, I'd sure do things differently! I'd appear first to my own flesh and blood. Then I'd march right over to Roman headquarters, straight into Pilate's office, and give the ol' boy the shock of his life. I'd certainly not entrust news of my destiny to a woman out of whom seven demons had gone!

But Jesus knows far better than I that the standards and approaches and power plays of the old creation are finished. There is no life left in these old ways. And when God does a new thing, when God brings forth life out of death, God chooses "what is low and despised in the world, even things that are not, to bring to nothing things that are" (1 Cor. 1:28).

So why do we in the church, the people of the new creation, continue to operate along the lines laid down for us by the old creation? Why do we continue to adopt and accept the entrenched distinctions of race, class, and sex? How can it be that Mary Magdalene, the first person to proclaim Jesus' resurrection, would not be allowed to share that news this morning from the pulpits of most churches?

But in Jesus Christ, God calls "Mary," Mary Magdalene, to be the bearer of the Easter tidings: "I have seen the Lord." When will we finally embrace her unexpected witness?

III

But the first command that the risen Lord gives to Mary is also unexpected: "Do not hold me" (John 20:17). We cannot hang onto Jesus as he may have appeared to us back in the '60s and '50s or the '40s and '30s. We cannot detain Jesus. We must follow him into God's future.

Did any of you see on Friday night the TV program on the Sisters of Charity? This Roman Catholic order of nuns has a special mission in nursing, in medicine, and in hospital administration. But only one woman a year is now entering the order. So the reporter couldn't help but ask the question, "What's going to happen when you are no more?" A nun, who administers a hospital with an annual budget of four hundred million dollars, replied, "Well, we're already preparing for that. Even now we're training lay people to take over from us and to continue our mission of mercy long after we're gone."

What an Easter outlook! Here and now those who witness to the new creation are letting go of the old for the sake of Jesus' mission. They know we can't freeze life. We can't bottle up grace. We can't cling to past experiences. We must let go of Jesus as he once was, for now he leads us in ways and to places we can scarcely imagine: "Do not hold me."

How do we release the past and step with Christ into the future? We make this move with Mary Magdalene because — unexpectedly — the Lord is risen! And the risen Lord is still calling unexpected witnesses like us. "Do not hold me," he says. For the Lord is going on before us, leading us in unexpected ways, into life eternal.

Second Thoughts about Easter

"Have you believed because you have seen me?
Blessed are those who have not seen and yet believe."
(John 20:29)

Today is often called "Low Sunday." Why? Is it because
church attendance is predictably low on this Sunday compared
to the Easter high? Or does "low" mean "low church" after
all the "high church" ceremonial surrounding Holy Week and
Easter Day?

Well, whatever the reason for Low Sunday, it suggests to
me that there are times in our common life when it is okay to
lie low, to kick back, to disengage high gear, to reflect on what
has happened and on where we are headed. Low Sunday is a
time for reflecting, a time for second thoughts — second
thoughts about Easter.

Our Gospel reading tells the story of the first Low Sunday.
A week after Easter, Jesus again appears to the gathered dis-
ciples. But this time, Thomas, who had not yet seen the risen
Lord, finally gets his turn.

Remember Thomas? Dubbed "doubting Thomas"? "Unless I see in his hands the print of the nails, and place my finger in the mark of the nails, and place my hand in his side, I will not believe" (John 20:25).

Do you know neighborhoods where you could walk into any bar and find skeptical, hard-nosed guys like that? Thomas obviously comes from Missouri — the "show me" state. A state that raises corn, cotton — and skeptics. If you say you're from Missouri, you're saying, "You've got to show me!" Thomas was from Missouri: "Unless I see . . . I will not believe." Low Sunday, indeed!

But, on second thought, one of the often overlooked themes in the Easter stories is the undercurrent of skepticism about the whole thing. Remember when the women tell the disciples the news of Jesus' resurrection? "These words seemed to them an idle tale, and they did not believe them" (Luke 24:11). Even when the risen Lord finally appears to these skeptical disciples, Luke reports that they still "disbelieved," albeit for joy (v. 41). It's just too good to be true. Matthew sketches the situation of Easter skepticism even more bluntly. He writes, "Now the eleven disciples went to Galilee, to the mountain to which Jesus had directed them. And when they saw him they worshiped him; but some doubted" (Matt. 28:16-17). Thomas is not alone in his doubts. Even in the very presence of the risen Lord, some disciples are still doubting.

We often think how easy it must have been for those first Christians to believe in the God of Israel, to believe that love is stronger than death, and to believe in Jesus' victory. After all, they saw the risen Lord. But on second thought, the appearances of the risen Lord are not convincing to all. "Some doubted." Apparently we belong to a community in which not everyone believes all the time. Apparently, we belong to a community in which, from the earliest days, doubt and faith coexist. Some disciples doubted — but they were *disciples*, nevertheless.

This is not to say that we delight in our doubts about Jesus' victory. But it is to say that we gather on the weekly anniversary of the resurrection not because we never doubt, but because of the promise that not even our doubts can "separate us from the love of God in Christ Jesus our Lord" (Rom. 8:39).

If the resurrection appearances of Jesus himself did not convince all the disciples all at once, then we are cautioned against putting more emphasis on these appearances than is warranted. "Have you believed because you have seen me?" asks Jesus of Thomas.

And in this gentle rebuke, Jesus suggests what the Gospel of John emphasizes throughout. Namely, that Jesus now comes to us as God's Word. Whenever this word is preached, the hour of decision is here. Whenever the word of Jesus is shared, faith hears in the ordinary words of ordinary people the message of new life from Jesus Christ himself.

That's why the Gospel of John makes no distinction between Jesus and Jesus' word. The saving power attributed to Jesus is also attributed to his word. For example, his words are "life" and "truth" (6:63 and 17:17); but so is Jesus himself (14:6). Whoever hears his word has "life" (5:24); but that is what Jesus himself is — "life" (11:25). His words (12:48; 17:8), his "testimony" (3:11, 32-33), are to be accepted — so also is he (1:12; 5:43; cf. 13:20). To reject him is identical with not accepting his words (12:48). That his own "abide" in him and he in them means the same thing as that his words "abide" in them (15:4-7). Thus, to encounter the living word of Jesus is to encounter the risen Lord himself.[1]

When will the word of Jesus come alive in you? Who can say? Jesus may become present to you long after you hear the sermon or receive the sacrament. Sometimes his word becomes activated in us by unexpected circumstances.

For example, Dr. David H. C. Read, as pastor of Madison Avenue Presbyterian Church in New York, once received the following letter from a parishioner:

---

1. See Rudolf Bultmann, *Theology of the New Testament,* trans. Kendrick Grobel (New York: Charles Scribner's Sons, 1951-1955), vol. 2, pp. 63-64.

Dear Dr. Read,

    After church today, late in the afternoon, I was walking out of my building on Gramercy Park and I heard a huge crashing noise. I looked to my right and I saw a young woman lying on the sidewalk. She had jumped from the neighboring building and had fallen through the canopy onto the pavement. She died on impact. The one other person who witnessed this went for the police. I stayed with the girl. No speculations ran through my mind as to how or why. Instead I felt a great sorrow for this young woman and for the enormity of despair she must have felt. When thought came through my feelings parts of your sermon came into my mind . . . a perishable thing raised imperishable; — sown as an animal body, it is raised as a spiritual body. I prayed that she be raised out of her human despair into the light of Divine love. . . .

    Your sermon this morning came to life in me this afternoon through tragic circumstances. The common bond between that which is perishable and that which is imperishable is love. . . . I want to thank you for the sermon you gave today. It helped make the incomprehensible tolerable through faith.

Today on this first Sunday after Easter, after all the crowds and glorious ceremonial, we confess that death and doubt are often more present to us than life and faith, that much of our experience is incomprehensible and, without Christ, even intolerable.

But the good news of the Easter gospel is that we do not have to fake it. The good news is not that everything always makes sense, but that in the non-sense God's Word still brings the risen Lord. The light is shining in the darkness, and neither our death nor our doubts can ever extinguish God's life and love for us in Jesus Christ.

On this Low Sunday, consider these second thoughts about Easter. Consider, on second thought, that even disciples doubt. Consider that the appearances of our risen Lord, while they count for something, do not count for everything. Most of all, consider that our risen Lord comes to us now through the word, clothed in his promises.

So amid our second thoughts about Easter, let the last word come not from the preacher, but from the Lord. For turning his body to Thomas, Jesus says, "Do not be faithless, but believing." Then, directing his words to us, Jesus gives his special blessing for Low Sunday, a benediction to all who cannot find visible evidence for faith: "Blessed are those who have not seen and yet believe."

Amen!

The Pattern of Recognition

Luke 24:13-35

Stories often have a moment of truth — what literary critics call a "recognition scene." Such moments of truth are the stuff of detective fiction and crime mysteries, as Agatha Christie, Dorothy Sayers, and Dick Francis well know. "Whodunit?" we ask. And at some point in the story our eyes are opened by some clue, and we recognize what's really going on. "Aha!" we say — with a little help, of course, from the likes of Hercule Poirot or Lord Peter Wimsey.

In the recognition scene, the story "clicks," the pattern comes together, and the end is at hand for the truth is disclosed. "Aha!" we say.

Because the Bible is a book full of stories, the Bible is full of recognition scenes. Remember Mary Magdalene? She stands outside the empty tomb of Jesus and takes her Lord for the gardener. Only when he calls her by name, "Mary," does she recognize him. Recognition scenes. The Bible is full of them.

And this morning we have from Luke yet another moment of recognition, of an Easter encounter.

> While they were talking and discussing together, Jesus himself drew near and went with them. But their eyes were kept from recognizing him. . . . When he was at table with them, he took the bread and blessed, and broke it, and gave it to them. And their eyes were opened and they recognized him. (Luke 24:15-16, 30-31)

The Lord, at table with fellow travelers, took the bread, blessed it, broke it, and gave it to them. And amid *this* action, *this* pattern, these events of *taking, blessing, breaking,* and *giving* — they recognized the presence of Jesus, the Jesus who had been crucified.

This fourfold pattern of taking and thanking, of breaking and sharing is at the heart of every celebration of the Lord's Supper. From the starkest Baptist memorials to the most sumptuous Byzantine commemorations, in revival tabernacles or city cathedrals, all celebrations of the Lord's Supper have a pattern by which Jesus Christ is recognized. The bread is taken, blessed, broken, and given.

This fourfold meal pattern, which comes to us from an ancient Jewish table blessing, really has two basic movements: a vertical movement of praise and thanksgiving to God and a horizontal movement of sharing bread — the basic stuff of life. Praise the Lord and pass the bread! This action was instituted by Jesus Christ himself as the permanent pattern for the community it constitutes. Such praising and sharing is the pattern of Jesus Christ whose life and death was "a continuous thank-offering to God." Whenever and wherever this pattern of thanksgiving to God and sharing with others occurs, Christ comes again, known once more in the breaking of the bread.

This pattern is not only the shape of our Lord's presence among us, but it is also the shape of the Christian life, that life to which our baptism calls us and to which we are to be conformed. Praising God and passing the bread — these are the marks of the people of God. In this pattern of thanksgiving and sharing, our Lord comes on the scene.

And when does our Lord come on the scene? Does he come only when we are ready, only when we have our act together, only when the church is finally decent and at last in order? Well, not according to the New Testament! For Paul records that the Lord comes to his supper "on the night when he was betrayed" (1 Cor. 11:23). He comes to his people amid their betrayals and denials. And he comes praising God and sharing his very life.

That first Easter evening, in an afterthought called Emmaus, people are pretty sad, and the word on the street is that Jesus and his cause are dead and buried. It is in such a time as this that the Lord appears on the scene; it is in such a time as this that the Lord becomes recognized; and it is in such a time as this that he comes to his own in the breaking of the bread.

And this is the good and great news about communion. We do not gather this morning to observe the Last Supper. We do not come to a funeral banquet. We gather solemnly, but joyfully, with eyes opened wide, at the table of the risen Lord. The Lord's Supper truly brings us Jesus Christ, not because we are good, but because God is gracious; not because we are all fixed up, but because, amid our rubble and ruin, God arrives on the scene.

What we celebrate today is neither magic nor merely symbolism and certainly not ritual for ritual's sake.

What we celebrate this morning is simply the way God chooses to be among us. God wills to be with us as we give thanks and as we share with one another. This is the pattern, the eucharistic pattern, by which Christ can still be recognized.

One crafter of modern recognition scenes, Flannery O'Connor, is remembered for her short stories. She was a practicing Christian, a Roman Catholic, who came from Milledgeville, Georgia, a place perhaps more obscure than even Emmaus.

Recalling a dinner party in New York, with the trendy and

the witty, Flannery O'Connor remembers her own recognition of the importance of communion:

> "I was once, five or six years ago, taken by some friends to have dinner with Mary McCarthy and her husband, Mr. Broadwater. . . . She departed the Church at the age of 15 and is a Big Intellectual. We went at eight and at one, I hadn't opened my mouth once, there being nothing for me in such company to say. The people who took me were Robert Lowell and his now wife, Elizabeth Hardwick. Having me there was like having a dog present who had been trained to say a few words but overcome with inadequacy had forgotten them. Well, toward morning the conversation turned on the Eucharist, which I, being the Catholic, was obviously supposed to defend. Mrs. Broadwater said when she was a child and received the Host, she thought of it as the Holy Ghost, He being the 'most portable' person of the Trinity; now she thought of it as a symbol and implied that it was a pretty good one. I then said, in a very shaky voice, 'Well, if it's a symbol, to hell with it.' That was all the defense I was capable of but I realize now that this is all I will ever be able to say about it, outside of a story, except that it is the center of existence for me; all the rest of life is expendable."[1]

Dear friends, if the Lord's Supper is only a ritual or just a symbol — why bother? "To hell with it!" But if Luke's story of the encounter at Emmaus is right, if thanksgiving and sharing form the pattern of God-with-us, then this Supper is the center of existence, and the decisive clue about the shape real life takes.

---

1. Quoted by Brian Moore, review of *Collected Works of Flannery O'Connor*, ed. Sally Fitzgerald, *New York Times Book Review*, 21 August 1988.

When he was at table with them he took the bread and
blessed, and broke it, and gave it to them. And their eyes
were opened and they recognized him. . . . Then they told
. . . how he was known to them in the breaking of the
bread.

Thanks be to God!

The Lion and the Lamb

Revelation 5

The Book of Revelation, with its visions of Armageddon and a new heaven, of seven spirits and seven stars, of seven seals and a scroll, has not shaped our faith and practice very much. And we are in good company!

Vast sections of the ancient church did not regard this book as Scripture. Luther's hesitations are on record. Calvin's are perhaps betrayed in that he wrote commentaries on every book of the New Testament — except Revelation.

In our own time, the last book of the Bible has not gained easy acceptance among the heirs of modernity. Its cosmology doesn't square with Astronomy 101. And isn't our egalitarianism scandalized by a vision of Jesus Christ that finds tattooed on his thigh, "King of kings and Lord of lords" (19:16)?

Despite the church's long distrust of Revelation, the book persists both in our canon and in our culture. And for the moment, that's all the warrant we need for the lion and the lamb of chapter five.

Scene One: The heavenly monarch holds in his right hand

a scroll fastened with seven seals. We later learn that this scroll tells the conclusion of the human story. When a strong angel with a loud voice asks, "Who is worthy to open the scroll and break its seals?" no one anywhere in the universe is found worthy (Rev. 5:2-3).

Scene Two: Our court reporter, the seer of Revelation, begins to weep uncontrollably. According to his account, "Then one of the elders said to me, 'Weep not; lo, the Lion of the tribe of Judah, the Root of David, has conquered, so that he can open the scroll and its seven seals'" (5:4-5).

Scene Three: No sooner has our elder stage-whispered to the stricken seer to expect the Lion of Judah, than who should appear but "a Lamb standing, as though it had been slain" (5:6).

We are told to expect the symbol of majesty,
    and we are given the symbol of meekness.
We are told to expect one who is sovereign,
    and we are offered one who has suffered.
We are told to expect the Lion of Judah,
    and we behold the Lamb of God.

Expect a lion, and what do you get? A lamb! Some comfort. What's going on here?

As I struggled with this text, an idea caught my fancy. Old Testament scholars often make the point that the promises of God are never fulfilled in predictable ways but always in ways that open up new possibilities on the horizon of history. Could it be that just as the coming of the Christ was the unexpected fulfillment of messianic vision, so, with the unexpected appearance of the Lamb, God's fidelity is not to be confused with our penchant for predictability?

While I find this interpretation intriguing, I do not find it convincing here. For when the lamb appears instead of the forecasted lion as the one who is worthy to take history in hand, neither the sobbing seer nor the comforting elder reacts with any surprise, shock, or confusion. It's as if the lion and the lamb have already become synonymous, that to behold the Lamb of God who suffered under Pontius Pilate is to behold the Lion of Judah who reigns and shall reign forever and ever.

Here we have a revising and redefining of ultimate reality.

For the God made known in Jesus Christ is one whose majesty is in meekness and whose sovereignty is in suffering. The one who is lionized is the living lamb who was slain. God's utter vulnerability is God's victory. In Jesus Christ, our seer perceives that the lion of justice and the lamb of love are not Jekyll and Hyde opposites in God but one reality. If this is true, then we have glimpsed a vision that contradicts those that still presume to govern our world.

For the world we so often experience is, on the one hand, a sentimental one, in which "love, sweet love" is proclaimed without regard to matters of deep injustice; or, on the other hand, a tyrannical one which liquidates "dissidents" or deports refugees, all according to the letter of the law, but without regard for mercy. Love without justice is sentimentality. Justice without love is tyranny. But in Jesus Christ we do not meet either sentimentality or tyranny, the enemies of our full humanity.

Some years ago, *The New York Times Magazine* carried a feature story by Nicholas Gage entitled, "My Mother Eleni: The Search for Her Executioners."[1] Gage's mother, Eleni, was a Greek peasant. She was one of thirteen villagers tried, tortured, and then murdered by communist partisans on August 28, 1948. According to her son, Eleni's only "crime" was to have smuggled him out of the village before he could be shipped by the communists to a "re-education" center. For this deed, she was executed.

Thirty-two years later her son, now a *New York Times* correspondent, quit his job and devoted all his efforts and savings to tracking down his mother's killer. In a story that reads like a spy-thriller, Gage penetrated layers of silence,

---

1. *New York Times Magazine*, 3 April 1983, pp. 20ff.

aliases, and false leads, and finally found the man who had ordered Eleni's execution, the feared Katis. Gage came upon Katis dozing in his comfortable seaside cottage, much as David — Judah's Lion — had once overtaken sleeping Saul.

Gage writes, "I stood staring at the man who had killed my mother, for a few minutes, perhaps more." But as he readied his revenge, Gage recalled how his "mother did not spend the last of her strength cursing her tormentors, but, like Antigone, she found the courage to face death because she had done her duty to those she loved. . . . Killing [Katis]," Gage confessed, would have given "me relief from the pain that had filled me for so many years. But as much as I want that satisfaction, I have learned that I can't do it. My mother's love, the primary impulse of her life, still binds us together, often surrounding me like a tangible presence. Summoning the hate necessary to kill [Katis] would have severed that bridge connecting us and destroyed the part of me that is most like Eleni."

Gage had pursued the truth about his mother and about her killer. Every dirty fact had been unearthed at last. Like a roaring lion he had ranged over Greece seeking to vindicate his mother's love. He had finally cornered the killer and confronted the truth. Justice was being executed — and then a moment of grace interposed. A love which would not let him go grasped him. A love which acknowledged ugly reality held him. A love which enlarged his humanity beyond the genuine need for revenge overcame him. And he acknowledged its sovereignty. Vindication took place by overcoming vindictiveness.

That's the God we discover in Jesus Christ.

The one who like a lion tracks us down, penetrates our disguises and our aliases, and confronts us with the unflattering truth about ourselves and our lives, not to devour us, not to destroy us, but to destroy all that dehumanizes and disfigures us.

In our text from Revelation, every creature in heaven and on earth and under the earth crowns the lamb with praise and thanksgiving. Yet we do not sense from the seer of Revelation that this universal shout of acclamation will be coerced or forced out of unwilling subjects. The victory of God is not in our compulsion but in our recognition that the Lamb of God who has stooped to shoulder his cross is the Lion of Judah who has our destiny in hand.

"To him who sits upon the throne and to the Lamb be blessing and honor and glory and might for ever and ever!" And the four living creatures said, "Amen!" and the elders fell down and worshiped. (Rev. 5:13b-14)

PENTECOST

The Promised Paraclete

"If you love me, you will keep my commandments. And I will pray the Father, and he will give you another Counselor, to be with you for ever, even the Spirit of truth, whom the world cannot receive, because it neither sees him nor knows him; you know him, for he dwells with you, and will be in you." (John 14:15-17)

In the name of the Father, and of
the Son, and of the Holy Spirit.

In ancient times, if you helped someone in need, you were known as a *paraclētos,* a "paraclete." A physician or a nurse at the bedside of a stricken patient is a paraclete. Likewise a preacher who brings listeners a word of encouragement is a paraclete (cf. Acts 2:40; 1 Cor. 14:3). And a counselor-at-law rushing to the defense of a client is also a paraclete. This is the courtroom image the Revised Standard Version has in mind when it translates the *paraclētos* of our text as "counselor."

Jesus Christ is our paraclete, a present help in time of

trouble. Sometimes we speak of his help in the language of medicine: he is our Great Physician; sometimes we use the language of law: he is our Advocate with the Father; and sometimes we use the language of preaching: Jesus is the Word, the encouraging Word of God. Jesus came on the scene to counsel a world that had lost its way. He came to bring life; he came not to condemn, but to save; he came as a paraclete, a helper.

But there's where the difficulty lies. For our text from John 14 arises out of a context — a context of anxiety. The ministry of the earthly Jesus is drawing to a close. The paraclete is leaving the scene. He is saying farewell to the disciples. He is returning to the Father. And in the face of his imminent departure, the disciples cannot help but wonder, "Well, now what?"

Does God give help only to take it away when we need it most? If the paraclete leaves our side, if God in Christ turns away from us, if his support is pulled out from under us, then how can we go on? Into this situation of anxiety over the future, a future seemingly bereft of help, Jesus brings this word of promise:

> And I will pray the Father, and he will give you another [paraclete], to be with you for ever, even the Spirit of truth. . . . (John 14:16-17)

Who is this Spirit, this Holy Spirit?

According to the Gospel of John, the Holy Spirit functions in ways that are parallel or identical to those of Jesus himself (5:30; 8:16, 42; 13:3). Jesus is sent by the Father; so is the Spirit (14:16; 15:26). Jesus as the Revealer of God is visible only to his own and not to the world at large (1:10, 12; 8:14, 19; 17:8); so also with the Spirit (14:17). As the Son of God teaches and leads into truth (14:16-17; 8:32, 40-42, etc.), so does the Spirit (14:26; 16:3). As the Son speaks not on his own account (7:16-17; 12:49-50), neither does the Spirit (16:13). As the Son bears witness to himself (8:14) and convicts the world of sin (3:20;

7:7; etc.), so the Spirit bears witness to Jesus and convicts the world of sin (15:26; 16:8).[1]

The Holy Spirit does today what Jesus did in his earthly ministry. And the Spirit does it as God with us and for us forever.

With this insight, the Gospel of John reframes the crisis in the church. The departure of Jesus is not the end of God with us and for us: "I will pray the Father, and he will give you another [paraclete], to be with you for ever, even the Spirit of truth. . . ." The Holy Spirit is for us what the earthly Jesus was for his disciples: a paraclete from God, a helper, a counselor, an advocate, a comforter — one who comes to our aid and defense in time of trouble.

The departure of the earthly Jesus now becomes the occasion for the sending of the Spirit. But the Holy Spirit does not come to displace Jesus or Jesus' teaching. The Holy Spirit only comes to magnify Jesus Christ. The Holy Spirit recalls for us his teaching, for the Holy Spirit is the Spirit of Jesus Christ sent at his request (14:16) and in his name (14:26). The Holy Spirit comes to our aid in a way that does not draw our attention from Jesus Christ. This Spirit only seeks the will and the way of the Son of God.

Who is the Holy Spirit? The Holy Spirit is the Spirit of truth who enables us to love. This Spirit enables us to love truly and to tell the truth lovingly.

We have a proverb in the American South: "Always tell the truth; but don't always be telling it." I guess that's a way of saying that truth is a greater burden than most of us can bear. We need all the help we can get to be both truthful and loving at the same time. We need a paraclete! And the promise of the parting Jesus is that there is a helper on the way who can enable us to live both truthfully and lovingly.

---

1. See Rudolf Bultmann, *The Gospel of John: A Commentary,* trans. G. R. Beasley-Murray (gen. ed.), R. W. N. Hoare, and J. K. Riches (Philadelphia: Westminster Press, 1971), pp. 566-67.

Some years ago a tourist was exploring a market street in Damascus, Syria. He watched as a bicyclist balanced a crate of oranges on his handlebars. Suddenly, a porter appeared, so bent with a burden that he didn't realize he was walking right into the path of the bicycle. Smack! Well, the oranges went rolling down the street, the burden was dropped, and a war of words broke out between the two men as a crowd gathered. Then the bicyclist moved toward the porter with a clenched fist. Just then, a tattered little man slipped out from the crowd. He took the raised fist in his hands and kissed it. The cursing stopped. The two men relaxed. The crowd murmured approvingly. People began picking up the oranges. And the little man, who helped the healing to happen, melted back into the crowd.[2]

Aren't there times in life when we, too, need some quiet counsel? when unintentionally we collide with others or find ourselves in unforeseen conflict? We don't always know what hit us, but we know we're in a mess. And when the oranges go rolling down the street, we know we need a paraclete, a present help in time of trouble.

And the promise of Jesus comes to us right at the point of our need. For there is a sweet Spirit who comes from God — a Spirit of truth, a Spirit of love, a Spirit whose kisses open clenched fists, a Spirit who helps us pick up the pieces, re-shoulder our responsibilities, and who gets us back on the road once more.

Jesus promises, "I will pray the Father, and he will give you another [paraclete], to be with you forever, even the Spirit of truth. . . ."

Come, Holy Spirit!

---

20. Kenneth W. Morgan tells this story, which I have paraphrased, in his letter to the editor, *New York Times*, 30 January 1991.

Who Is My Mother?

Joshua 2 and 6
Matthew 12:46-50

"Who is my mother?" Jesus asks (Matt. 12:48). A rhetorical question, no doubt. But still, a strange one!

"Jesus, excuse me. Your mother is that woman standing just outside, patiently waiting to see you now that you're a celebrity."

"Jesus, need we remind you, your mother is the one who, amid scandal and later at risk of her life, brought you into the world."

"Who is my mother?"!

Would it ever occur to us to ask such an impertinent, mocking question?

We know who our mothers were and are. Those women whose names are typed on our birth certificates or adoption papers, whose snapshots grace our dressers, or whose portraits hang in our halls. Women who gave us our first home, hummed many a lullaby, told us Bible stories, and who, after a long day of work, still summoned love and time for us.

And then this disrespectful question, "Who is my mother?" gives way to an equally unexpected answer. For with Mary nearby, Jesus stretches his hands toward his disciples and declares, "Here are my mother and my brothers!" explaining that "whoever does the will of my Father in heaven is my brother, and sister, and mother" (Matt. 12:49-50).

What's going on here? To help us move from Jesus' question, "Who is my mother?" to his answer, "Whoever does God's will," I would like for us to recall — with some imaginative license — a story in the Book of Joshua about a woman named Rahab.

*   *   *

It had been a long day and Rahab, the innkeeper, was just beginning to light the lamps in her tavern. Perhaps the name of her inn was "Tavern in the Wall," because the walls of her inn were identical with the outer walls of the city of Jericho. Like so many other prostitutes in the Ancient Near East, Rahab was a kind of barmaid in the business of providing lodging, companionship, and pleasure for weary travelers.

Earlier that day, while Rahab was cleaning her tavern, several miles beyond the Jordan, the supreme commander of Israelite forces, Joshua, was planning a secret spy mission with his intelligence officers. If all went well, Joshua hoped to plop two Israelite agents right in the city of Jericho itself, his next military objective. Can you picture Joshua, an ex-spy himself, poring over maps of Jericho — that famous walled fortress city just seven miles north of the Dead Sea and commanding the River Jordan?

Going over the city block by block, street by street, Joshua marked the key gates, the sentry posts, the lookout stations. Questions filled his mind. How large was the garrison? Was morale high? Were stores stocked for a siege? To find the answers to these and other questions he had to place his agents inside those city walls. But how? Slowly an idea began to form.

Yes! That was it! Tavern in the Wall!

It was a perfect "cover."

Who would ever think of finding Israelite spies in a whore-house? Travelers — all men — frequented these inns often. Who would even notice or care if two random travelers just happened to stay there this evening? And who would even suspect their real mission? And so it was that 007 and 008 were summoned to Joshua's field tent. By afternoon, these two agents were sneaking off to Jericho.

The spies approached the city late in the day. The gate was still open, and a long caravan stretching for miles was just approaching the welcoming portal. Pulling their cloaks tightly around their heads, amid the dust and jostling camels, 007 and 008 passed undetected into the city. Within minutes, they were standing at Tavern in the Wall, the first arrivals of the evening.

As Rahab looked up from lighting her lamp, two pairs of strange eyes greeted her. She went through the formal motions of welcome, sizing up her guests in the process. She had never seen these men before. They spoke the language of Jericho, but with a trace of accent new to her. She poured the wine.

While 007 and 008 were quaffing their wine, little did they know that a trap was about to spring on them.

You see, the king of Jericho was a most resourceful monarch. He had an intelligence-gathering capability of his own. Word had reached him from a double agent, a mole, operating in Joshua's camp, that Israelite spies were even now arriving in Jericho. What is more, they were lodging with Rahab the harlot.

Rahab happened to look out her window and noticed that police were cordoning off her block. When she looked out her back window, the one in the wall of Jericho, she saw a detachment drawing up. Then she noticed something else. The look of panic in the eyes of her guests.

For reasons we do not know, Rahab quickly led the two strangers to her roof. On its flat surface, fresh cut flax was drying. Motioning for the men to get down, she hurriedly covered their bodies with grain. Rushing back downstairs, Rahab reached her bar counter just as the Jericho SWAT team flung open the tavern door.

"Where are they?" an officer demanded. Rahab feigned ignorance. "The men that have come to you, who entered your house; for they have come to search out all the land" (Josh. 2:3).

Cleverly guessing that an out-and-out denial would not convince, Rahab told a half-truth.

"True," she said, "men came to me, but I did not know where they came from" (v. 4); yes, that much was true.

But then she told the lie.

"And when the gate was to be closed, at dark, the men went out; where the men went I do not know; pursue them quickly, for you will overtake them" (v. 5).

The lie worked. Eager to catch the spies before they got away for good, the soldiers tore out of the city, racing to the Jordan fords as the city gates swung shut behind them.

Now Rahab knew something she had not known before. Something very important. She now knew who these mysterious strangers were. Spies. Israelites. They were scouting out Jericho to prepare for an attack. Rahab now knew a great fear, and, at the same time, a new faith. As she later confessed to her hidden house guests,

> "We have heard how the LORD dried up the water of the Red Sea before you when you came out of Egypt, and what you did to the two kings of the Amorites that were beyond the Jordan, to Sihon and Og, whom you utterly destroyed. And as soon as we heard it, our hearts melted, and there was no courage left in any man, because of you; for the LORD your God is he who is God in heaven above and on earth beneath." (vv. 2:10-11)

In fear and trembling, amid the recognition that in these spies the Lord had paid the harlot a house call, a way to freedom began to emerge. She had saved the lives of the spies. Now they owed her one. And being a shrewd woman, wise in the ways of the world, Rahab persuaded the Israelite agents to spare not only her life, but that of her father and mother and brothers and sisters! The plan was simple. When Joshua's army entered Jericho to unleash its annihilating fury, Rahab would see to it that a scarlet cord was hanging from her window. By prearrangement this would be the sign that all in her tavern were to be spared the sword. The deal struck, Rahab helped the two spies out of her window in the wall.

And when the walls of Jericho finally came tumbling down, and the Israelite troops scrambled over the rubble to finish off the inhabitants, a scarlet cord was dangling in the ruins. That ribbon of red led Joshua's men to Rahab and her household huddling in the wreckage awaiting their promised rescue.

And so concludes our story. "Rahab the harlot, and her father's household, and all who belonged to her, Joshua saved alive; and she dwelt in Israel to this day, because she hid the messengers whom Joshua sent to spy out Jericho" (Josh. 6:25).

Have you got the picture? Here is Rahab, perhaps aged and wrinkled, but still alive after all these years in the land of Israel. Picture a distinguished, highly honored senior citizen, decorated by her adopted country, living with dignity, surrounded by children and grandchildren, a heroine of the invasion of Canaan.

*   *   *

Who is my mother?

According to tradition, based on Matthew's genealogy (1:5), Rahab the Jericho harlot was the great-great-grandmother of King David. Rahab was a direct ancestor of Jesus of Nazareth!

But even if this tradition is not literally true, even if Rahab had never married and never reared children, she would still be found where she is today among the heroes and heroines of faith enumerated in the eleventh chapter of Hebrews: "By faith Rahab the harlot did not perish with those who were disobedient, because she had given friendly welcome to the spies" (v. 31).

Yes, Rahab would still have been a mother and sister to Israel, and a mother and a sister to our Lord. For she did the one thing needful: at a particular moment, in a particular place, in a concrete set of circumstances that shock our modern sensibilities, *she did the will of God*. This is how the harlot became a mother to all Israel and to all the world.

What impresses me about the story of Rahab is its suggestion that we can never know God's will in advance of the concrete situation in which it overtakes us. Our tendency is to want to nail down God's will in a list of truths, or rules, or commands.

Take honesty for example. My great-grandfather was a small-town druggist. His business failed, largely because a trusted employee stole him blind. A friend once commented, "Mr. Kay, you are just too honest for your own good." A reticent person, Kay quietly answered, "There is no such thing as being too honest." Surely, to be honest and truthful is to do the will of God. Surely, we can know that much in advance. But here is Rahab also doing God's will by telling a lie.

Take patriotism. Surely, patriotism is another valiant and important virtue. "For God and Country" is the theme we inculcate into our church Boy Scout troops. But here is Rahab also doing God's will by betraying her country, long before Dietrich Bonhoeffer betrayed his, Nazi Germany, in the name of Jesus Christ.

Not only does the will of God redefine who is our mother, it redefines all sorts of things — such as truth, such as patriotism.

So while we can never know the will of God in advance, all neat and tidy, all nailed down for time and eternity, Rahab also reminds us that the will of God does overtake us and call us to new faith and new life in the strangest places — even in pagan Jericho, even in a whorehouse. And sometimes, the will of God breaks in upon us even in church, of all places! There really are no walls thick enough to keep the will of God from finding its way through them.

The story of Rahab tells us that God comes to meet us in the mayhem. When all the walls that define reality come tumbling down — amid the mess, the mixed motives, the rubble of our lives — God can meet us. And that red ribbon of mercy and grace can still guide us through the agonies and disasters that life can bring. For that red thread runs from Rahab's tavern window tying all who follow it to Jesus Christ. His word of life creates a new people, not based on blood or on soil, but on the will of God.

Who is my mother? Whoever does God's will. And if Jesus Christ is right about this, then he, too, must be my mother — and brother and sister — for in him the will of God lives today. And today he invites each of us to join with Rahab the harlot in saying yes whenever and wherever God's will and way overtake us.

Burnout — and Beyond

1 Kings 18 and 19

When did you last stand on the summit of success? Was it the morning the postal worker delivered a letter admitting you to your first-choice college or university? Was it the afternoon your boss announced with a smile that you had been made a partner of the firm? Or was it the candlelit evening when the one standing beside you turned and said, "I do"? In such memorable moments, success is so real and so present that we can practically taste it. How sweet it is!

These moments of success are not foreign to the Scriptures. Moments when things long amiss finally turn out all right, when the only thing to do is to join in singing with Deborah about Israel's victory over Jabin, in feasting with Queen Esther at Purim in the shadow of Haman's gallows, in killing the fatted calf, eating, and making merry because the prodigal son who was lost is now found. If you have ever had one such moment of success — when things turn out right — you can also identify with the prophet Elijah standing victorious on Mt. Carmel.

Remember the story? How Israel's Queen Jezebel was busying herself exterminating the morality, the worship, and the prophets of the Lord God? How Elijah single-handedly challenged Jezebel's 450 prophets of the sky god Baal to a contest on Mt. Carmel?

"You call on the name of your god," Elijah bellowed out to them, "and I will call on the name of the LORD; and the God who answers by fire, he is God" (1 Kings 18:24). Well, "from morning until noon," the prophets of Baal cried out for their god in ritual dance, in bloody self-flagellations, raving even as Elijah taunted them. "But there was no voice; no one answered, no one heeded" (vv. 26, 29).

Then Elijah rebuilt an overturned altar to the LORD and poured water three times over the waiting sacrifice until the ground around the altar was soaked and the moat around the altar was filled. And then, astride Mt. Carmel, Elijah prayed:

"O LORD, God of Abraham, Isaac, and Israel, let it be known this day that thou art God in Israel, and that I am thy servant, and that I have done all these things at thy word. Answer me, O LORD, answer me, that this people may know that thou, O LORD, art God, and that thou hast turned their hearts back." Then the fire of the LORD fell, and consumed the burnt offering, and the wood, and the stones, and the dust, and licked up the water that was in the trench. And when all the people saw it, they fell on their faces; and they said, "The LORD, he is God; the LORD, he is God." (vv. 18:36b-39)

What a moment! What a God! What a prophet!

Baalism broken! Jezebel's prophets killed with the same fury with which she had slain those of the Lord God. Her domestic policy was in shambles. Elijah on Mt. Carmel couldn't be more on top of the world! And as the smell of the consumed sacrifice filled the air and became the smell of success, how sweet it was!

In the face of this moment which is still affecting the course of our civilization, the only thing to do would be to celebrate this great victory of the Lord God over the powers that had taken Israel captive. But instead of celebration, within just a few hours of this summit of success, Elijah, our text informs us, "was afraid" (19:3). Afraid of whom? Afraid of what?

The dramatic events of Mt. Carmel did not convince Queen Jezebel. The Lord God of Israel may have overpowered her prophets, but she was not moved — except to avenge their deaths. She sought Elijah's life. She wanted him dead within twenty-four hours. And what Jezebel wanted she usually got. And so, the day's success notwithstanding, Elijah "was afraid."

In panic, Elijah's fear turned to flight. "He arose and went for his life, and came to Beer-sheba, which belongs to Judah" (19:3). Elijah, the same Elijah who had fearlessly faced down the prophets of Baal, was now on the run. He crossed the frontier into Judah heading for the desert, a fugitive from victory.

And alone in the desert, bitter despair overwhelmed him. Within only hours the story of Elijah takes us in panic all the way down from the peaks of success to the desert depths of defeat and despondency. The voice that had awakened and troubled all of Israel now can only whimper in weakness: "It is enough; now, O LORD, take away my life; for I am no better than my fathers" (19:4). The man of the hour was not celebrating. He only wanted to curl up under a broom tree and die.

Why? Surely, the wrath of Jezebel could have been no greater than the potential dangers Elijah faced on Mt. Carmel. What had happened — and, apparently, so quickly — to disable such a gifted and giving prophet of the Lord? Does our text suggest the root cause of Elijah's despair — and perhaps our own? When the Lord overtook Elijah now holing up in a desert cave like a trapped animal, Elijah let loose with his pent-up complaint. And in this complaint the reason for the fear, the flight, and the despair becomes much clearer:

"I have been very jealous for the LORD, the God of hosts; for the people of Israel have forsaken thy covenant, thrown down thy altars, and slain thy prophets with the sword; and I, even I only, am left, and they seek my life, to take it away." (19:14)

"I, even I only, am left." So sure. So self-righteous. And so self-destructive!

The temptation of those who are gifted and giving is to believe that they are indispensable to the work of the Lord. As I look out on this congregation this morning, I am looking at commitment. For it takes some doing to get to church on a hot summer Sunday to hear some preacher no one knows about. And because I suspect that commitment to the work of the Lord is rather strong among summer churchgoers, Elijah reminds us that our peculiar temptation — precisely because we are here — is to regard ourselves, and perhaps only ourselves, as utterly indispensable: "I, even I only, am left!"

Where do we get this idea that we are so indispensable — that God has no other hands but mine; that God has no other eyes but mine; that God has no other servant but me alone? Where do we get this presumptuous notion? For gifted and giving persons who persist in this notion, every success calls forth new and fearful stresses, the accumulative weight of which leads to the pit of despair. "I, even I only, am left!" — and then comes the crack-up or the burnout.

So convinced was Elijah that he was indispensable to the work of the Lord, so self-absorbed had he become, that our text reveals a terrible irony. Of course Jezebel did not believe in the God of Mt. Carmel, but did Elijah? In a sense, he was as faithless as Jezebel because he forgot that he was not the source of God's victory. No wonder he was terrified. No wonder he was utterly despondent. For in the end, he only looked to himself. Those who wish to be indispensable, as only God can be, damn themselves to despair.

But God had something to say to Elijah. And God has

something to say to each of us who believe that we are God's golden boys or golden girls, that we alone can right wrongs, rescue others, or save impossible situations.

To the despairing cry, "I, even I alone, am left," the Lord replied that he was keeping "seven thousand in Israel, all the knees that have not bowed to Baal" (19:18).

We can almost hear the Lord saying, "Elijah, you're not alone. But you've become so fixated on your own abilities and contributions that you haven't noticed others who are remaining faithful under desperate conditions. They haven't given in. They haven't given up. They've moved beyond burnout, because they've learned the ever-new lesson of Mt. Carmel that only I, the Lord, am God; only I am indispensable. They've moved beyond burnout, because they've moved beyond the faithlessness that says, 'I, even I only, am left!' Elijah, while you languish here in the desert, I've got seven thousand back in Israel who have bowed neither to Baal nor to burnout because they've bowed to me."

To say "The Lord is God" is to confess that I am not God, that God's purposes are bigger than my psyche, that I am not indispensable to the coming of the kingdom. Indeed, the Lord made this all very clear by accepting Elijah's resignation. True, there were a couple of jobs the Lord still wanted Elijah to undertake, but one of them was to anoint Elisha as his successor.

For those in the depths of despair who, like Elijah, cry for release from destructive expectations, our God is the God who gives comfort and rest. If in a national emergency, when the question of Israel's very survival was at stake, even Elijah could resign, the God who does not leave himself without a faithful witness can accept our resignation as well. So tendered, it can also be a sign to our frantic, activist culture that God reigns. It is better to fall on our faces crying "The Lord, he is God" than to drop to our graves under the illusion that we are!

But how much better it would be to acknowledge that the Lord alone is God before we reach the point where we are crushed under the illusion of our indispensability.

A few months after a riot in south-central Los Angeles, I interviewed a young minister and his wife, Roy and Lois Smith, who were serving a small, struggling, interracial congregation.

The problems were staggering. Three thousand children were growing up within a few blocks of the church in a neighborhood where drugs were as easy to buy as bread. Once in broad daylight, Roy watched a thief break into his house, and twice in the same year his car was stolen. But into this setting Roy and Lois came lighting their gospel lamps, and soon, a host of social service programs were started.

I'll never forget a remark Roy made to me in our interview. When I asked him if he weren't afraid for his safety, he quoted to me these words of David Livingstone, "I am immortal until my work is finished." Then he added, "We have found that you can't minister and be afraid."

This is faith's freedom — from fear and from despair: to know that the Lord is God. Only when I lay down the impossible burden of my indispensability am I truly freed to speak a prophetic word, enact compassion, or live a *human* life. Only in the God-given freedom from playing God can I know the joy of genuine ministry to others. This is what converts boasting into prayer and bragging into praise. This is what transforms brittle moralism into lives of thanksgiving. And this is what brings us back from the brink of burnout — over and over again — to the worship of the true and living God!

"I, even I only, am left"? No! May we join with that "remnant, chosen by grace" (Rom. 11:5) to declare not only with our lips but in our lives that "the Lord, he is God! The Lord, he is God!"

Lord, Give Us the Word!

I charge you in the presence of God and of Christ Jesus who is to judge the living and the dead, and by his appearing and his kingdom: preach the word, be urgent in season and out of season, convince, rebuke, and exhort, be unfailing in patience and in teaching. . . . always be steady, endure suffering, do the work of an evangelist, fulfil your ministry. (2 Tim. 4:1-2, 5)

My colleague at Princeton, Tom Long, recently reported to the faculty about a conference on evangelism held in Charlotte, North Carolina. Tom had just returned from this conference where he spoke on preaching and evangelism.

Tom had flown to Charlotte out of Newark. After parking his car at the airport, he waited at a curbside shelter for a shuttle bus to the terminal. Here Tom fell into conversation with a businessman bound for a sales meeting in Chicago.

"Where you going?" the businessman asked.

"Charlotte," Tom replied.

"Going on business?"

"Yes."

"What kind of business?"

"Well, I'm a professor, and I'm going to give a lecture."

"Sounds interesting. What are you lecturing about?"

"Theology."

"Theology? What sort of theology?"

"Preaching."

"Oh, thank God," replied the businessman. "I thought you were going to say evangelism!" Then he added, "I'm sick to death of evangelists."

Yes, many are sick to death of evangelists. And many more are sick unto death because of them. So we hesitate to use terms like "evangelism" or "evangelist." We are sick to death of what those words have come to represent.

Nevertheless, the "Paul" of the pastoral Epistles charges Timothy: "Do the work of an evangelist" (2 Tim. 4:5).

What do evangelists do anyway? Part of our confusion is that when we hear the term "evangelist," we automatically imagine a revivalist. But it has only been in this century that revivalists have become styled as evangelists. Only in this century did the term "evangelism" become synonymous with "revivalism."

So when Paul, centuries ago, charges Timothy to "do the work of an evangelist," he is not commanding Timothy to give altar calls or to market the Messiah. Rather, Paul is commanding Timothy to preach and teach the evangel, the gospel, the good news, of Jesus Christ.

We cannot resolve here the broader question of whether in the New Testament an evangelist is the office of only some Christians or the activity of all. But we can say that if sharing the gospel is the calling of every Christian, this calling still comes to focus in the pastor. "Do the work of an evangelist," Paul charges Timothy, the pastor. And in Paul's exhortation, the work of an evangelist is understood as preaching and teaching: "Preach the word . . . be unfailing . . . in teaching" (4:2). I want to say a word on behalf of preaching.

We are facing an emergency situation in many churches. Word percolates back to the seminaries that pastoral nominating committees simply cannot find effective preachers. One seminary board of trustees has become so alarmed by this trend that they are threatening to hold the homiletics faculty personally responsible for the failings of their students. (That certainly got my attention!) But I wonder, are nominating committees willing to give pastors the untrammeled time in which to think, to read, to craft their sermons? We cannot have it both ways. We cannot expect vital preaching if we overburden pastors with incessant demands for fund-raising, administration, program development, counseling, calling, and community involvement. Since there appears to be little letup in these demands, we'll probably not recover effective preaching until we recover an effective diaconate. But in this unseasonable time for the pulpit, Paul declares to us, as he declared to Timothy, "Preach the word. . . . Do the work of an evangelist."

What is this word we are to preach — in season and out? In Paul's exhortation, the term we translate "preach" carries the connotation of a herald running ahead of a royal entourage. Whenever heralds cry out royal proclamations, they do not do so on their own behalf or on their own authority; neither are they simply crowd pleasers. Far from it! Heralds only announce what their monarch authorizes. Likewise, we who preach, who herald the gospel, do not invent it every Saturday night. It is given to us.

In this sense, every preacher is a kind of Margaret Tutwiler. Remember the State Department spokeswoman often seen on TV during the Gulf War? Ms. Tutwiler only announced what the State Department authorized. Her own opinion, even her personality, was irrelevant. What mattered to the world was her message — the message she was given to say. Similarly, Paul can write to the Corinthians, "We are ambassadors for Christ, God making his appeal through us" (2 Cor. 5:20). This is consistent with Luke's account of the commissioning of the seventy. Jesus says to them, "He who hears you hears me" (Luke 10:16). And this is why the Second Helvetic Confession can boldly declare: "The Preaching of the Word of God is the Word of God." Through the mouths of his heralds, the Lord speaks — and still speaks today. Therefore, "Preach the word. . . . do the work of an evangelist."

But what is this word God has authorized? Paul calls it the "word of the cross" (1 Cor. 1:18), or "the word of life" (Phil. 2:16), or "the message of reconciliation" (2 Cor. 5:19). However described, this word we preach is the message of what God has done in Jesus Christ. The story of Jesus, as the decisive clue to our destiny, is the evangel we preach. Thus, the preacher of the word has a very different task from that of Margaret Tutwiler. For the Word of God is never a frozen formula. Preaching the gospel is not chanting code words, even great ones like "Lord, Lord." Nor is preaching the gospel simply reminiscing about the life and times of Jesus of Nazareth. Preaching the gospel unpacks the story that this Jesus loved us and gave himself "for us," "for many," and, hence, "for all." And this word, this gospel we are to preach, "is the power of God for salvation to every one who has faith" (Rom. 1:16).

Is that true? Is God's Word that sovereign? that compelling? that transforming? If it is, then why does the "Paul" of the pastorals use such forceful language to get Timothy to preach this Word? Why is that? If God's Word is so powerful, why is Timothy so timid? So fearful? So discouraged? And why are we?

Why is that?

My teacher, Jim Forbes, used to say, "We preachers have to get called — and then we have to get re-called."

Why is that?

The poet Robert Bly muses about the wife who "looks at her husband one night at a party, and loves him no more. The energy leaves the wine, and the minister falls leaving the church."[1]

Why is that?

Such discouragements are reminders that God's Word, like the love of a friend or a spouse, is never our possession. It's always a gift. God's Word is neither a thing we control nor a magic trick we conjure up. God's Word is a living encounter for which we can only pray. As Paul says, "No one can say 'Jesus is Lord' except by the Holy Spirit" (1 Cor. 12:3).

Do you know what I mean? You receive a phone call late at night. A troubled young man hints pretty clearly that he is going to take his life. And so you pray, "Dear God, give me the words. Life hangs in the balance. Help me to choose my words. Help me convey your love for this tormented person." To choose our words in this spirit may well mean refraining from chirping our favorite code words into the telephone.

And on Sunday morning is it any different? Amid all the "Lord, Lord" talk rolling off our tongues, there they sit — people in desperate need, people at the brink of death — and, if the words are right — on the verge of life. We must choose our words. We must preach the word. But only God can give the word of life. Lord, give us the Word!

Toni Morrison's haunting novel *Beloved* knows a thing or two about the Word and a thing or two about life. In her story, there is a marvelous woman revivalist named "Baby Suggs." She is a great preacher: "Love is or it ain't," she says. "Thin love ain't love at all." Not bad for one who was "uncalled, unrobed, and unanointed." But late in her life Baby Suggs grows despondent. Overcome by a series of tragedies, she gives up on preaching. Then one of her friends comes and pleads with her: "You can't quit the Word. It's given to you

---

1. Bly, *Iron John: A Book about Men* (Reading, Mass: Addison-Wesley Publishing Co., 1990), p. 82.

to speak. You can't quit the Word, I don't care what all happen to you."[2]

We "can't quit the Word"! Not because we are good, or even pious. But we "can't quit the Word," because it still comes to us from on high and grasps us with its truth and power. And we "can't quit the Word" because, through the likes of us, some named Timothy and some named Baby Suggs, those who hear us will yet hear their Lord.

"I charge you in the presence of God and of Christ Jesus who is to judge the living and the dead, and by his appearing and his kingdom: preach the word . . . do the work of an evangelist, fulfil your ministry."

"You can't quit the Word. It's given to you to speak."

Lord, give us the Word!

---

2. Toni Morrison, *Beloved* (New York: Alfred A. Knopf, 1987), p. 177.

ALL SAINTS' DAY

It Does Not Yet Appear

Beloved, we are God's children now; it does not yet appear what we shall be, but we know that when he appears we shall be like him, for we shall see him as he is. (1 John 3:2)

Every fall, for as long as anyone can remember, students have poured into Princeton. But no sooner do you get your futons unrolled, your PCs on-line, and your textbooks cracked than it seems you are repacking your trunks, loading your U-hauls, and moving on to something new. Every spring, sitting through commencement, I wonder — what will become of you? Much of the time, it does not yet appear what you will be.

My high school graduating class recently held its twenty-fifth reunion. There was Mary Ann. She'd been kicked out of the marching band for some infraction. But today she is a concert pianist, well known in Scandinavia, and with a budding international following. There was Doug. Doug was a skinny kid who sat next to me in biology. We spent much of our semester injecting male chickens with testosterone. The idea was to discover if this growth hormone really made chickens bigger. While Doug held the terrified, wiggling chick, my job was to inject it. This was not as simple as it may seem. You would not believe the evasive action a chicken can take. One time, I jabbed the syringe intended for the chick right into my own thumb. I have no idea if this had any permanent effect upon my growth — biological or otherwise. What I *have* discovered since that semester long ago is that my laboratory sidekick is now an honorable judge. About the time Doug turned thirty-five, when most lawyers are just hanging out their shingles, he was appointed to the bench. More often than we might think, "it does not yet appear what we shall be." We just do not know what will become of us.

If we could travel back to the winter of 1789 in Frankfurt, Germany, we might meet a young theological student named Fred. He has finished his formal academic studies in theology. Predictably, he is now "filled with skepticism and resignation." His reddened eyes and knotted stomach tell the story: he is now preparing for his ordination exams. Fred has six weeks to submit his papers. He must give an exposition of Christian freedom as set forth in the fifth chapter of Galatians. He must also answer the question, "For what purpose does a future Christian teacher study polemics?" Then, he must take up such questions as "the essence of Hebraic poetry," "the natural powers of human beings," "the chief translations of the Old Testament," and discuss the kind of books that the beginning theologian should read in order to pursue a successful career. Finally, Fred must preach on Luke chapter five before a group of seasoned pulpiteers. No wonder he has stinging eyes and stomach cramps! When the grades come back, Fred's work in dogmatics is judged only satisfactory; what we used to call a "gentleman's 'C'." But *this* mediocre student in dogmatics became the founder of modern theology. We have long forgotten the name of his examiners, but the towering mind of Friedrich Schleiermacher continues to challenge theology even today.[1] "It does not yet appear what we shall be." We simply do not know what will become of us.

But is this really all our text is claiming? Do we have here simply another plug for possibility thinking? Is the gospel of Jesus Christ really reducible to a truism you can find in almost any self-help book?

Don't we know all too well what we shall be? It's November 1st — winter is coming. And as we shuffle and slosh our way over carpets of rotting leaves, mortality is all about us. In the Northern Hemisphere this is the season of death and dying. No amount of clock-changing can hide that fact. This is the time for ghosts, and goblins, and rattling saints — relics long departed, but somehow strangely near.

Someday we too shall fall like leaves. We too shall fade away. Cut off from life, we too shall surely die. We too shall become unclean and impure. Whatever our attainments, our friends and families will walk by on the other side of that ditch that separates the living from the dead. Strangers will come with their plastic gloves and their plastic bags and haul us away. We shall be buried, or scattered, and forgotten. This is our lot. This is our destiny. It *does* appear what we shall be.

But in the face of mounting evidence, our text answers, "No." "It does not yet appear what we shall be."

Is our destiny something we can see so clearly and know so completely that we can print it out in laser sharpness? Not for those who are God's children now!

Is our destiny something we can plot or predict on the basis of present trends? Not for those who are God's children now!

For the gospel questions all our assumptions about what will be — not because it has a precise picture of what eternity looks like, but because it knows of a Lord who brings us the promise of all things new, what John calls "eternal life."

---

1. On Schleiermacher's student years, see Martin Redeker, *Schleiermacher: Life and Thought,* trans. John Wallhausser (Philadelphia: Fortress Press, 1973), pp. 17ff.

"It does not yet appear what we shall be, but we know that when he appears we shall be like him, for we shall see him as he is." Out on the horizon of the future, Jesus is coming to meet us. The shape of the human family, the shape of the church, has not yet appeared in final form, because there is more to come from Jesus Christ. In the words of Christopher Morse, "What we shall be is not yet *in* hand, but it is *at* hand."

That is why we who are God's children now can never take our own projections as seriously as God's promises. If the future were not Jesus Christ, but simply the sum total of present trends, death and dissolution would win every time. But because Jesus Christ is our future, we can be God's children now.

Can it be? Is it true? The more we surrender our plans and prognostications and the more we trust in God's power to appear in ways we could never foresee, the more we are becoming, here and now, like our Lord who is coming to meet us. That's the testimony of the saints.

Recently, I opened yet another piece of "junk mail" from denominational headquarters. What saved this letter from the "round file" was the return address. It included two names I recognized — Don and Patsy Mullen. My junk mail actually turned out to be their open letter:

> During the last year at Princeton Theological Seminary, along with a full load of classes, Don was President of the Senior Class and passed the Ordination examination of the Presbyterian Church. Patsy was busy auditing classes, traveling back and forth between Charleston and Princeton and continuing to be the mother of five adult children. It was a very intense year. . . . Since leaving the practice of cardiovascular surgery in Milwaukee three years ago . . . *we did not realize what such a major transition in our lives would mean.*

Yes, "it does not yet appear what we shall be." Our degrees, whether M.Div. or M.D., are not the final index by which our destiny is known. What we do know is that we are God's children now. What we do know is that Christ is our future.

Between his final exams in May and commencement in June, Don Mullen flew to northern Iraq. There in the squalor of Kurdish refugee camps, under the most appalling conditions, this Milwaukee surgeon treated three to four hundred people a day with the medicine of mercy.

Yes, "it does not yet appear what we shall be," and we do not realize all at once what God's future will mean. But in the sacrifices of such sisters and brothers as Patsy and Don, and in all the saints who have looked to Christ, we see our crucified Lord drawing near to meet us.

Thanks be to God!